The Boeing 747

The Boeing 747

David H. Minton

TAB AERO

Blue Ridge Summit, PA

Aero series

40

FIRST EDITION
SECOND PRINTING

Library of Congress Cataloging-in-Publication Data

Minton, David.
   The Boeing 747 / by David H. Minton.
     p. cm.—(Aero series ; v. 40)
   Includes index.
   ISBN 0-8306-3574-2
   1. Boeing 747 (Jet transports) I. Title.
TL686.B65M57 1991
629.133'349—dc20   90-21315
                        CIP

TAB Books offers software for sale. For information and a catalog, please contact TAB Software Department, Blue Ridge Summit, PA 17294-0850.

Acquisitions Editor: Jeff Worsinger
Book Editor: Steven H. Mesner
Production: Katherine G. Brown
Book Design: Jaclyn J. Boone
Cover photograph courtesy of Boeing Commercial Airplane Group.

Contents

Acknowledgments

I would like to acknowledge support from the following: Boeing Commercial Airplanes, McGraw-Hill, Aviation Data Center, *Kit Collectors Clearinghouse*, and *Airliners* magazine.

Introduction

T HIS BOOK is for you if you are an airliner observer, historian, or modeler, or if you have any interest in the Boeing 747. It covers all variants of the 747 in use, including military and civil versions, both American and foreign. It discusses the origins of the design and the evolution of the 747 into a "world class" airplane like no other—probably the single greatest contribution in modern times to allowing the people of the world to meet and mingle.

Beginning as a "wide-body" jet in a class all its own from the start, the 747 has evolved into one of the most sophisticated, complex, and cost-efficient aircraft ever built. It carries more people farther than any other aircraft in existence. This book chronicles the history of the magnificent 747, while along the way, pointing out some of the colorful and significant historical events associated with it, including records, terrorism, and accidents. Many of the most colorful schemes ever put on a 747 are illustrated, together with a fleet listing. Finally, the book covers virtually all of the models of the 747 available, with construction, conversion, and livery tips provided for many of the most important.

In short, if you are interested in the 747, this book has something in it for you.

1

In the Beginning

L IKE ALL Boeing airplanes, the Model 747 began with an idea. For the 747, the largest commercial jet in service, the idea was to meet a requirement yet unborn, a requirement foreseen in certain people's imaginations—not yet a reality, not yet discovered. The basic issue concerned projections for air travel in the 21st century.

These projections heralded *more*: a lot *more* travelers and a lot *more* cargo using the same airports and the same airplanes. Some people envisioned an almost steady "airplane conveyer belt" of people being transported in and out of airports using conventional airplanes. Day and night, the sky would be full of airplanes as people arrived and departed. More airplanes of existing types were not the answer, because each airplane could hold only so many people, so more airplanes would simply get in the way. More airports wouldn't help, because people wanted to go to the same basic destinations. There was simply no place to put more airports.

Bigger and Better

If more planes and more airports wouldn't meet the need, then the answer had to be bigger airplanes. And, in Boeing's case, bigger implied a lot bigger. When the Boeing 747 was first conceived, the largest intercontinental airliner in service was the Boeing 707, which could carry up to 200 people (depending on configuration). It could fly to any international airport in the world and was in service, at that time, with approximately 70 different carriers throughout the world. The 747 was envisioned as the 707's replacement, but able to fly farther, faster, higher, and carry up to 500 people at a time—over twice as many per aircraft as the 707. In addition to relieving the overcrowded skies, this aircraft offered the possibility of lower operating costs per passenger, since the same four engines would be carrying more than twice as many people. When all is said and done, the operating cost per passenger is perhaps the single most important consideration to the passenger carrier.

1

*Pan American was the first to order the 747 and has used them since the beginning. Seen here in that carrier's most recent markings, with the titles in large letters in Pan Am blue on the fuselage in lieu of a cheat line, N740PA, **Clipper Ocean Pearl**, a series 121, makes her way across the skies.*

All carriers (with the exception of government-owned or subsidized carriers) are in business to make a profit and stay in business. In a sense, because airlines were more regulated when the 747 was first conceived and fuel was a lot cheaper, the profit incentive was not as magnified as it is today. But it was still a major consideration, as was passenger comfort, which promised to be much better on a two-aisle wide-bodied jet.

Regulation had been a natural fallout of the original subsidy of the airline companies to carry mail. In the beginning, the U.S. government was the largest customer of the carriers, paying for the transportation of mail, by air, across the United States. With the Air Mail Service (as it was then called), a letter could get from New York to San Francisco in about 20 hours, with an average of 18 stops along the way, whereas surface mail (by train) could take up to three days. Passengers were included more by accident than by design. The carrier would have a contract with the U.S. Government to pay for the specific route, and any additions or extra freight—passenger or otherwise—that was carried just happened.

As it became apparent that the ground service requirements for aircraft were just as important and expensive as the aircraft itself, the involvement of the government in terms of services and safety became more and more complicated. In this sense, "ground service" included much more than just refueling and loading the jet; it also provided for all of the runways and terminals, all of the landing and instrument aids, and all of the various navigation aids that were slowly springing up across the United States. In the meantime, passengers began to provide real income to the carriers, and carrying the mail and other government merchandise slowly became of secondary rather than primary importance to most of the carriers. The airlines began to evolve.

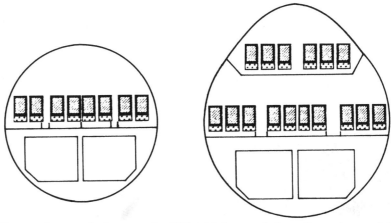

The difference in capacity between the 747, with its two deck configuration, and the nearest similar capacity wide-body aircraft, the DC-10, is illustrated here. The 747 can carry about six times as many passengers as the original DC-9 and a little less than twice as many as the DC-10 illustrated here.

BOAC (British Overseas Airways Corporation), later British Airways, was one of the early operators of the 747. Seen here with the gold speedbird on the tail, NM12799B was later delivered as G-ANNA.

But it was easy for the government to slip from the position of being the primary customer to subsidizing the various carriers to develop and provide incentives for air travel. Therefore, the public began to get a deceptive idea of the *true* cost of air travel. From the very beginning, carriers had a real idea of their *real* operating costs, and the proposed Model 747 offered a simple way to decrease these costs. A decrease in costs translated to an increase in profits—the ideal proposition for carriers. Under deregulation, the cost subsidy of the fare structure for the individual carriers would be removed. With this removal,

The 747, largest of the Boeing jetliners, can carry over six times as many people as the Boeing 737, smallest of the Boeing jetliners. Here the first Western Airlines 737 series 200 is seen in the original Indian Head markings.

the actual cost of the fare would become more important. Unfortunately for the carriers, cost is driven much more by the total operating expenses—including the Direct Operating Expense (DOE)—than one might expect. Thus, if a carrier has a domicile in New York and a domicile in San Francisco, the total cost of operating a modern jetliner between

In actual use, the 747 has more directly replaced the intercontinental 707s, widely in use at the time the 747 was first delivered. Detractors claimed the 747 was nothing but a scaled-up 707, but history would prove them wrong. Seen here is OD-AFT, a 707 in MEA markings, with the Cedar of Lebanon on the tail.

those two destinations will be less than between two destinations for which there is no domicile. The reason for this is that all of the ground handling expenses are already included at the domiciles, *whether or not* the aircraft arrives, but they must be leased or bought from some other carrier or service agency at other destinations. So a ticket from New York to San Francisco might be half the cost of a ticket from New York to Salt Lake City and a fourth of the cost of a ticket from Albany to Butte for the same carrier. The actual distance is not really that much involved in cost, particularly after a certain threshold of about 500 miles.

But the new 747 would require an entire new generation of ground handling and service equipment. This consideration was somewhat threatening to the carriers, so the task of selling the 747 was not as simple as it could have been. Indeed, all of these considerations were included in the life-cycle cost estimates developed by the Boeing engineering team. Also included, but not obvious, were the production costs, which would require an entire new generation of hangars and assembly facilities and techniques.

With all of these facts in hand, the 747 engineering team estimated the cost per aircraft at 20 million in current dollars. They estimated a break-even cost of about 50 aircraft. The initial study was, in effect, bootstrapped from an earlier government competition for the CX (later to be known as the C-5 series, which Boeing lost to Lockheed), so by this time, most of the technical facts for the 747 were already in hand. The C-5 was a government-developed and sponsored aircraft, and was the first true jumbo jet to fly, even though it has never been made in a passenger version.

Although Boeing lost the government transport contract, it decided to test the water for a commercial version of a similar aircraft. Armed with multiple artists' conceptions of the finished plane in the respective carriers' livery, and various facts and figures, the team set off on a tour of various international airline companies. They visited airline facilities

While not a direct competitor of the 747, the Douglas DC-10 was sold as a wide-bodied transport. Many carriers operate both 747s and DC-10. Here a British Caledonian DC-10 is seen at Long Beach in the delivery markings on a maiden flight. The DC-10 can carry about 225 people depending on the configuration.

throughout the world, often running into teams from Douglas, who at the same time was working on the DC-10 project, and teams from Lockheed, who was working on the L-1011 project. It was as if an entirely new generation of wide-bodied jets suddenly took hold at the same time.

First Orders

In the beginning, Boeing received what was then the largest order in the history of commercial airliners. Pan American Airlines placed an order for 25 of the new Boeing 747s, at a total cost, including spares, of over $550 million. Armed with this single order, the Boeing engineering team began serious work on the remaining design effort, the goal now being to build and fly a Boeing 747. Slowly but surely, the aircraft took shape under the team's hands. After trying a variety of fuselage configurations and shapes, including double passenger configurations, the rather strong, simple lines that we have come to know all over the world emerged. These lines did not change shape in the ensuing months.

Another aircraft sold as a wide-body was the Lockheed L-1011. This Eastern Airlines white-crowned Whisperjet is seen enroute. The L-1011 also carries a maximum of about 225 people.

Because of the increase in the cockpit height—now some 30 feet from the ground—Boeing pilots were concerned that there might be problems with learning to ground-handle the aircraft. This led to the invention of a simulated cockpit, mounted high above a truck bed, for the purposes of familiarization. Thus, as the engineering crews were working on the prototyping and fabrication of the actual aircraft, the flight crews were evolving a whole new generation of cockpit simulators, which would eventually impact the entire concept of flight training and associated costs.

Similar problems, owing to the 747's increased height, were met and solved concerning the evacuation process during emergencies. New, larger galleys to feed more people had to be designed. Entirely new entertainment systems—with up to four different movies showing at the same time in different parts of the aircraft—had to be developed.

The implementation of the 747 required an entirely new family of ground handling and servicing equipment, as can be seen by the various pallets and loading equipment surrounding this Northwest Orient 747 in Honolulu.

Boeing already had experience with a double-decker fuselage design. One of the most successful transcontinental airliners in post-WWII service was the Boeing 377 Stratocruiser, a double-decker airliner built on the basic B-29 airframe. The double-decker arrangement for the Stratocruiser was a "double-bubble" affair. Such a design was considered unacceptable for the 747, which would be traveling at speeds much higher than those of the 377. One of the early problems was where to put the crew. There were several interesting designs proposed, including the so-called "droop-snoot," in which the upper cabin deck tapered quickly down to the nose, where the cockpit crew was located. In all, more than 50 different variations of the double deck fuselage were seriously investigated by Boeing for the 747. Eventually, however, the elegant design we know so well today was adopted.

Many of the early development aspects of the 747 were finalized with feedback from its potential eventual users, the pilots and cabin crews of the carriers who ordered the aircraft. There are many interesting anecdotes about changes to the galley door locations, increasing sizes in drains, and redesigning the spiral stairs associated with the design of the first 747. By the time the new 747 design was ready for customer input, Boeing was adept at putting these ideas into practice.

Above all, Boeing designed the aircraft with safety in mind. There is, in some systems, *quadruple* redundancy to ensure that, as Boeing puts it, "no single failure will jeopardize the passengers, crew, or cargo."

Orders for the aircraft continued to grow. As Pan American announced adding the new aircraft to their inventory, it seemed they almost challenged all other carriers to join them in ushering in this new age of wide-bodied aircraft. The challenge seemed to work, and the other carriers quickly responded. Soon after the initial Pan Am order, orders started coming in from all over the world, with Lufthansa, long a faithful Boeing customer, becoming the first non-U.S. carrier to order the big new jet. Orders eventually

In addition to new cargo-handling equipment, the 747 required a new generation of food and cabin service equipment, as can be seen servicing this Swissair 707-300.

came in from Delta, Eastern, Aer Lingus, Continental, Japan Airlines, Air Canada, World Airways, KLM, United, American, Air France, Alitalia, BOAC, and Swissair. Today, virtually every noncommunist country has at least one 747 flying international routes, primarily between their capitals and London, New York, Los Angeles, Tokyo, and similar cities. Japan Airlines has as many as 60 of the jumbo jets, with an additional 20 on order, and currently has the largest fleet of 747s in the world (a position long enjoyed by Pan American until recent years).

First Flight

Finally, the first 747 was ready to fly. The maiden flight, which lasted about 45 minutes, was uneventful. As Boeing noted in its in-house newsletter, it was almost anticlimactic that the aircraft ushered in a new era of wide-bodied transportation. Pilots were satisfied with the overall handling characteristics of the aircraft. After a couple of landings and takeoffs, the "tall" cockpit location seemed almost natural to them. There were none of the scary problems associated with the Boeing 727 program, in which pilots were often disoriented by the relationship of the aircraft to the ground and sometimes flew the plane into the ground on landing. Although the 747 was obviously different in this relationship,

Although designed for containerized cargo, the 747 can easily handle a variety of palletized cargo, as seen being loaded on this KLM white-crowned series 100 somewhere in the far east.

the extensive training and familiarization required by the program more than compensated for the size of the new aircraft.

Best of all, from the point of view of the engineering team, pilots *liked* the new jet. They were quick to learn its handling characteristics both on the ground and in the air. The use of the rear steering on the main struts made the aircraft almost as easy to handle on the taxiways as smaller jet airliners, according to pilots who flew both types. And the 747's flight characteristics were quickly applauded. No one expected the plane to be as smooth and easy to handle as it was on its very first flight. All parties concerned were eager to get the 747 into service, but several problems were yet to come.

The 747 has been known by a variety of interesting names. The largest of Boeing's jets, it has shared the name "Fat Albert" with the smallest of Boeing's airliners, the 737 (see Aero Series 37, *Boeing 737*, TAB book No. 20618). It has also humorously been referred to as a "condominium" and a "flying tin heap." With the advent of newer series 747s, the older ones have been called "classics." But from the very beginning, the Boeing 747 was different, larger, more stately—"The King of the Road."

Aer Lingus

Aer Lingus put the 747 to work on international routes between Dublin, Shannon, and New York. Seen here is **St. Colmcille,** *which was leased to Air Siam shortly after delivery. Markings are the early light and dark green on a white crown.*

Airliners via J. Wegg

The 747 SP, or Special Performance, is a smaller, long-range version of the 747. Typically, it can carry about 100 fewer passengers than a series 200, but can travel about 1000 miles farther. This red-trimmed Air Malawi SP, 7Q-YKL, is seen in temporary service in 1985.

2

In Development

D URING the Second World War, visual aircraft recognition was extremely important. Aircraft recognition and observer's books were published to help people learn the quick detection of an aircraft throughout the war and for some considerable time thereafter. Although the Boeing 747 came long after such books ceased to be published, a recognition manual might have described the 747 as follows:

"Easily the most widely recognized passenger aircraft in the world, the 747 is a two-story affair with a cockpit bulb on the top front. The wings are instantly recognizable, shaped like a boomerang and tucked low in the belly of the enormous fuselage. From the cantilever wings are hung huge engines, dwarfed only by the yet bigger size of the aircraft."

But a simplistic description such as this, while perhaps visually describing the aircraft, belie the vast technology and flexibility embedded in it. Boeing was quick to realize that the 747 was, in a real sense, a plane for all seasons in the long-haul business. True, a 747 could not get from London to New York as fast as the Concorde, but the fact of the matter is that there is very little call for service such as is available on the Concorde, even if it is all First Class. Most passengers would rather pay a considerably lower fare and arrive at their destination somewhat later. The transit time from London Heathrow to New York Kennedy is about three hours on the Concorde and about six hours on the 747, depending on the time of the year, the weather, and so forth. However, because much of the total travel time is used up in getting to and from the airport, the actual improvement the Concorde offers in terms of total travel time is fairly small. As the distance travelled gets greater, the Concorde becomes more efficient, because it easily flies twice as fast as

The easiest way to distinguish a series 100 747 from later variants is by the number of windows at the top. Here, in original delivery "Friendship" colors, is a three-window United series 100.

the 747—but it cannot carry sufficient fuel to take full advantage of this capability. The Concorde must make frequent stops for refueling along the way, which naturally slows the aircraft down, and these takeoffs and landings add to the fuel burn, making it even more inefficient. On the other hand, the 747 can fly the distance. It has been in the business of setting distance records since its beginning. Additionally, Boeing has consistently increased the distance capability of the aircraft throughout its life.

Two Basic Versions

There are two basic versions of the 747, passenger and cargo. For both versions, once the enormous infrastructure of passenger- and cargo-handling facilities and equipment is in place, it is easy to move enormous loads of freight from one hemisphere to another and across continents. Humans, being the peculiar beasts that they are, still prefer to travel at what might be called "convenient hours." That is, they prefer to take off about mealtime and arrive about mealtime. The ideal schedule is rumored to put the aircraft out at about the proper time for some specific meal, or have it arrive just before some specific meal. For example, flying from San Francisco to Washington Dulles, a takeoff serving breakfast or lunch, with a landing just before lunch or dinner, is most desirable to passengers. In actuality, it might be that many of the flights are tied to work days, with arrivals and departures scheduled, as much as possible, to coincide with the beginning or end of the work day. Hence, those hours that are "inconvenient" to the passenger, as long as they don't cause problems with noise abatement, are available to cargo—and the 747 can carry a lot of cargo.

Boeing, having learned this early on in the 707 program, began to develop two different (but not independent) series of 747 aircraft, all-cargo and convertible passenger/cargo, in addition to the all-passenger version. While the cargo version wanted to carry a lot of freight, and the convertible version wanted to carry a lot of passengers and freight, the passenger version wanted to go farther and farther. This led to the creation of the SP, (Special Performance) version of the 747. From a passenger's point of view, the SP is probably the premier aircraft of all time. Because it is basically a downsized version of a regular 747, it can go higher, farther, longer, and faster than virtually any other passenger aircraft in service today. It also gets off the ground and above bad weather much faster than any other aircraft. But more importantly, it can follow those long and tremendous routes farther and faster than any other aircraft. Thus, carriers such as Qantas, South African, Iran

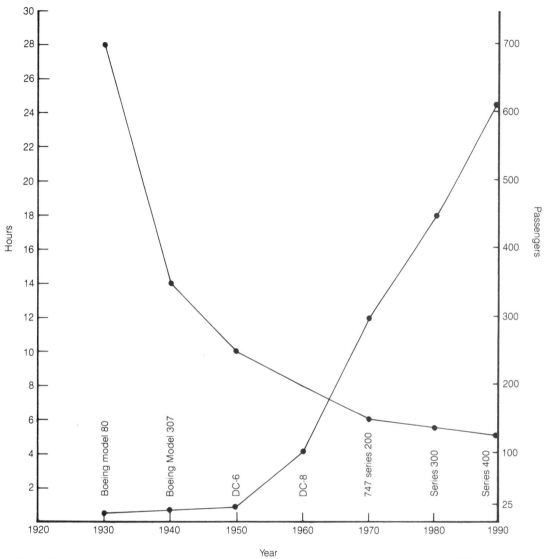

Graph illustrating distance vs passenger-carrying capacity by years for various aircraft for a trip from San Francisco to New York.

Air, and others who have to fly long routes between such cities as London and Cape Town or New York and Sidney were quick to recognize the use of such an aircraft. Other carriers (such as TWA and LUX) attempted to use the aircraft effectively, but were unable to support their markets. Nonetheless, Boeing aggressively developed and marketed the aircraft, and Pan American set records and developed excursion flights based on it.

For those carriers needing more passenger density over a shorter route structure, Boeing developed the SR (Short Range) version. The special seating arrangement for this aircraft allows seating for 498 passengers, (about half as many as the bullet train). Japan

The all-cargo version of the 747 is easy to recognize by the fact that the windows are completely removed from the aircraft. This Seaboard World Aircraft is now in service with Trans America.

The series 200 is easy to tell from the series 100 by the number of windows at the top—10. This aircraft, called "Big Orange" because of the color, was also known as "747 Braniff Place," and for a number of years was one of the most elegant international addresses.

Airlines put this version to work on the very densely traveled Tokyo-Osaka and Tokyo-Sapporo routes. This particular use of the aircraft closely parallels one of the early reasons for the 747's development: to provide for more people on fewer planes.

For the cargo version, Boeing went to the heart of the matter and developed an aircraft that could easily carry 100 tons of cargo from point to point. Cargo carriers such as Seaboard, World Airways, and Flying Tigers were early to recognize this capability, and put the Boeing to work. World Airways in particular made much use of both the cargo and convertible versions. Other, more traditional carriers began to use the aircraft to replace their aging cargo fleet, so names such as Northwest Cargo and Pan American Cargo and JAL Cargo became common on the sides of the 747. Available for both regular and special (or charter) flights, these versions of the 747 have been seen at virtually every jetport in the free world.

Big Top and Megatop

Later, as the technology continued to evolve, Boeing developed a bigger and better aircraft. By the time the series 300 was put together, engines had become so efficient that it was possible to carry bigger and better loads farther and faster. The original series 300 was called (by carriers such as Singapore) the "Big Top," because it was basically a 747 with more advanced avionics and a bigger bulge on the top for the passengers. When Singapore put the series 400 into service, even though the fuselage was the same size, they called it the "Megatop."

It's not *quite* a double-deck version of the aircraft, but it is getting close. It is interesting to note, with ever-increasing fuel prices, the greater emphasis placed on the upper deck of the 747 as a passenger space. In some early versions of the aircraft, this space was little more than a passenger lounge. But from the series 100, with upper deck seating for 16, has evolved the new series 400, with upper deck seating for 84 in business class and 124 in tourist. Boeing offered carriers a chance to retrofit their series 100 aircraft to series 200—and later, 300—standards.

Trying to unravel Boeing series numbers can be quite a struggle. Originally, the aircraft was called, simply, the 747. However, as improvements were incorporated, the new aircraft was called the 747B. This implied that the original aircraft was the 747A. The convertible version of the aircraft was called the 747C, and the freighter version the 747F. However, it was quickly realized that the 747B was a different aircraft from the 747A. After a time (and certainly without any consistency), Boeing designated the new aircraft a series 200 and the original aircraft a series 100. This was something of a compromise

Boeing Commercial Airplanes

The series 300 is easy to recognize from the earlier series by the extension of the top, called both the SUD (Stretched Upper Deck) and the EUD (Extended Upper Deck). The series 300 has about twice the upper windows of the series 200. Seen in the new Qantas colors, this aircraft is on a test flight.

Many of the series 100 aircraft have been retrofitted to series 200 configuration with the addition of the upper deck seating. This NWO conversion at Log Angeles International shows to good effect how this conversion is implemented.

The series 400, the newest member of the 747 family, is easy to recognize because of the extended wings and the upturned winglets for long-range efficiency. Singapore put the series 300 into service as the "Bigtop." Later, when the series 400 entered service, it was called "Megatop." The series 400 has the same extended upper deck as the series 300.

between the designation of the series for the 707 and for the 727. With the 707, as different engines became available, the series was identified differently. For example, the 707 series 100 and 200 were powered by Pratt and Whitney JT3C turbojets, while the series 300 was powered by Pratt and Whitney JT3D turbofans and the series 400 by Rolls Royce Conways. Thus, to a great extent, you could determine the delivery engines from the

The Special Performance or SP version of the aircraft is also easy to pick out in a crowd because it is much shorter than the original version, and comes to a sharp taper at the vertical tail. Here, an American Luxury-Liner SP taxis out.

series number. With the 727 and 737, however, both of which were powered by Pratt and Whitney JT8D turbofans, the series number came to be a means of telling the *size* of the aircraft. In both cases, the series 100 was physically shorter than the series 200. With the 727, this never changed. With the 737, the aircraft went on to a new generation of series 300/400/500, all of which retain the original basic shape but which are powered by General Electric CFM 56 engines.

Putting the Custom in Customer

For the 747, however, this has not worked out the same. In a general sense, the series number tells you the size (i.e., the gross weight) of the aircraft. Because most of the aircraft customers use different engines, you will usually need more information than the series number to determine the engine type. The basic features of each series are identified below:

Series	Wingspan	Length	Passengers	Range
100	195ft. 8in. (59.64m)	231ft. 4in.	490	3721nm
SP	195ft. 8in. (59.64m)	183ft. 4in.	360	5933nm
200	195ft. 8in. (59.64m)	231ft. 4in.	516	6150nm
300	195ft. 8in. (59.64m)	231ft. 4in.	624	5650nm
400	211ft. (64.3m)	225ft. 2in.	680	7000nm

For the first couple years, nearly all 747s were delivered with Pratt and Whitney engines. Later, to meet specific carriers requirements, the General Electric or Rolls Royce engines were retrofitted. Continental inaugurated service between Los Angeles and Hawaii using the 747, called the "queen" of the fleet.

At the end of each series, Boeing has historically added a two-digit customer identifier for each specific customer. This number has remained the same across all Boeing aircraft lines. Thus, for example, 21 is the Pan American designator, and a 727-121 would designate a short-bodied 727 originally ordered and built for Pan American. In reality, because of options and trades, to say nothing of cancellations, such as aircraft could actually be delivered to anyone. Listed below are the two-digit customer designators for all of the original 747 orders. As you will recognize, some carriers never took delivery of their aircraft.

Designator	Carrier	Designator	Carrier
06	KLM	43	Alitalia
12	Singapore	44	South African Airways
17	Canadian Pacific	45	Seaboard World
21	Pan American	46	Japan Airlines
22	United	47	Western Airlines
23	American	48	Aer Lingus
24	Continental	51	Northwest Airlines
25	Eastern	56	Iberia
27	Braniff	57	Swissair
28	Air France	58	El Al
29	Sabena	73	World
30	Lufthansa (Condor)	83	SAS
31	TWA	84	Olympic
32	Delta	86	Iran Air
33	Air Canada	90	Alaska Airlines

Designator	Carrier	Designator	Carrier
35	National Airlines	98	Air Zaire
36	British Airways	B4	Middle East Airlines
37	Air India	D1	World Airways
38	Qantas		

For example, a 747 series 400 delivered to British Airways would be designated as a 747-436, and so forth. From this more-or-less heuristic scheme, you cannot determine the engine configuration unless you also know more about the carrier. British, for example, has a preference for Rolls Royce engines.

In the meantime, new technologies concerning wing construction using composite materials and wing efficiencies using tip fins were being developed. These technologies and others were eventually incorporated into the development of the series 400 aircraft. The series 400 is basically the original series 300 aircraft with a more extended upper cabin and new wing features that allow it to fly more efficiently with the same engine capability. The series 400 gave Boeing the chance to breathe new and current technology into a respected airframe. This new technology would be a balance between new avionics (including digital instrumentation and CRT displays) and the new wing concept. The result was a very extended upper fuselage with a deep upper deck for passengers. This is not truly a full two-deck aircraft, such as the C-124, but rather an extended upper deck for passengers along with a full lower deck. This allows for configurations with multiple cabin, business, and first class passengers. It must be recognized that we have grown so accustomed to the 747 that we fail to notice improvements. The fact is that "The King of the road" must—and does—compete with itself. With the advent of the series 400, the new life infused into the airframe took the form of intense competition among carriers; as with the series 100-to-200 and the series 200-to-300 upgrades, Boeing has provided for series 300-to-400 upgrades.

Besides having no cabin windows, the freighter version of the 747 has a forward-opening cargo nose, as seen on this Northwest aircraft, somewhere in Europe.

This flat polar view of the world lends itself to illustrating the tremendous range of the series 400 Boeing 747 centered on major gateways throughout the world. In this view, arcs are drawn from San Francisco, New York, London, Honolulu, New Delhi, and Melbourne showing the normal range of a standard series 400.

Although Eastern ordered the 747 early on, none were ever delivered. Eastern's aircraft instead went to other carriers. However, some aircraft were leased from Pan Am and put into service on Atlanta-Miami-Bermuda routes. This series 100 has the later engines in service.

Significant milestones in the development of the 747 are noted below:

Milestones in Boeing 747 Development

Boeing looses C-X competition to Lockheed.	Aug 1964
Boeing beings to sell 747 concept to international carriers.	July 1965
Pan American orders 25 747s.	14 April 1966
First Boeing 747 flown.	October 1969
Series 100 receives FAA Type Certificate.	30 December 1969
Series 100 put in service by Pan American New York-London.	21 July 1970
Series 200 first flown.	11 Oct 1970
Series 200 receives FAA Type Certification.	22 Dec 1970
Series 200 put into service by KLM.	Jan 1971
747C (Cargo) (Series 100) version first flown.	30 Nov 1971
Cargo (Series 200) version receives FAA Type Certificate.	7 Mar 1972

Cargo version put into service by Lufthansa.	14 April 1972
SR (Short Range) version first flown.	June 1973
SR version receives FAA Type Certificate.	July 1973
SR (Short Range) version put into service by Japan Airlines.	Oct 1973
SP (Special Performance) version first flown.	4 July 1976
SP (Special Performance) version receives Type Certificate.	4 Feb 1976
SP (Special Performance) version put into service by Pan American.	1 May 1976
Series 300 first flown.	5 Oct 1982
Series 300 receives FAA Type Certificate.	7 Mar 1983
Series 300 put into service by Swissair.	28 Mar 1983
Series 400 first flown.	24 Apr 1988
Series 400 receives FAA Type Certificate.	9 Jan 1989
Series 400 put into service by KLM.	Summer 1989

3

In Detail

I MPROVING the most successful airliner ever built has been both a challenge and a joy. Considered by many to be an instant classic, the Boeing 747 was designed from the very beginning to easily accommodate changes and improvements. In addition, it was crafted to be custom-tailored to the specific needs of individual customers.

True, the cantilever wings are low in the fuselage and are swept back like a boomerang, but they also house the most advanced triple-slotted flaps yet developed. The 747's engines are not just enoromous; they are the largest and most effective engines yet used on a commercial aircraft. There are several types of engines used on the aircraft, depending on the particular needs of the customer. Listed on page 24 are the major engine types used on the 747 and some of the typical customers for those types. As the 747 has developed, up to the series 400, the range of the aircraft has increased. Thus, as British Airways noted on delivery of the new series 400, except for Australia and New Zealand, all points on its route structure can now be reached nonstop from London!

Engines

Although the 747 was originally certified with the Pratt and Whitney JT9D-1B engines, these demonstrated unsatisfactory reliability. Subsequently, all Pratt and Whitney-powered 747s were retrofitted with JT9D-3As. Although the Pratt and Whitney engines were developed specifically for the 747, the aircraft was later certified for use with both General Electric and Rolls Royce engines. This keen level of competition has ultimately benefited the 747 passenger, because the end result has been delivery of an aircraft powered by an engine with substantially reduced fuel costs per passenger mile (one of the most important yardsticks used by airlines to measure potential profits). Although by no means comprehensive, TABLE 3-1 identifies the most significant of the engines in use on the 747, as

Flying in formation with the **City of Everett**, *the original 747, the new 747 series 400 shows its greater upper cabin expansion and wingtips to advantage.*

Boeing Commercial Airplanes

Table 3-1. 747 engines and their power and use.

Engine	Static Thrust (in pounds)	Series
Pratt and Whitney		
JT9D-1	41,000	100/200
JT9D-3/3A	43,500	100/200
JT9D-3D	45,000	100/200
JT9D-3W/3AW	45,000	100/200
JT9D-7	45,500	100/200
JT9D-7A	46,250	SP
JT9D-7R4G2	52,500	200/300
JT9D-7F	48,000	100/200
JT9D-7W	47,000	100/200
JT9D-70	52,000	100/200
JT9D-7R462	54,750	300
PW4056	56,000	400
PW4256	56,750	400
General Electric		
CF6-45A2	46,500	100/SP
CF6-50D	51,000	100/200

CF6-50E	52,500	100/200
CF6-50E2	52,500	200/SP/300
CF6-80C2	59,000	300/400
CF6-80C2B1	56,700	200/300/400
Rolls Royce		
RB211-524B	50,000	100/200
RB211-524D	53,000	100/200
RB211-524B2	50,100	SP
RB211-524C2	51,600	200/300
SPRB211-524D4	53,110	300
RB211-524D4-B	53,110	200/300
RB211-524G	58,000	400

well as the type of 747 and engine power. Other wide-bodies—for example, the DC-10 series 30—are powered by the General Electric CF6 type engine, while the series 40 is powered by the Pratt and Whitney JT9D type engine. On the other hand, the Lockheed L-1011, which sold to British Airways, is powered by the Rolls Royce 211 series engine.

The particular engines are not identified by the series, as has been the case with earlier Boeing airliners. The engines are specific to the requirements of the customer, just as are the internal seating and galley layouts.

Landing Features

Besides the electronic landing equipment on the 747, which will be discussed separately, the landing features can be divided into two major components: wing and flap assemblies and landing gear. The 747 comes with a more-or-less conventional wing—certainly so by today's standards—but with several innovations.

Pan American Airlines

Orange and yellow sun on the tail, National was one of the early users of the 747. N77772, a series 135 named **Patricia,** *was sister ship to N77773, named* **Linda,** *during the controversial "fly me" ads.*

The wing is a cantilever type, with triple-slotted flaps at the trailing edge and both Kruger and variable-chamber flaps at the leading edge. The variable-camber flaps, in ten separate sections, are outboard along the leading edge. They do not vary in camber until fully extended, and are made of a lightweight core material (which also has flexible characteristics) called "honeycomb." Although commonly used on aircraft today, when first introduced on the 747, the technology was new. Inboard, there are two sets of Kruger flaps. On each wing there are a total of six honeycomb spoilers, four of which are outboard for flight use and two of which are inboard and for ground use. In addition to the flaps, both low-speed and high-speed ailerons are located on the trailing edges of the wing at conventional locations.

All 747s except for the SP have this basic configuration. The SP wing does not feature triple-slotted flaps; rather, it uses an even more conventional single-slotted variable pivot type. Additionally, most of the wing substructures on the SP are made from lighter and/or composite materials, which contributes to the aircraft's longer range capability.

For the series 400, the basic wing discussed above was extended an additional six feet at each tip, and a vertical winglet also extends up six feet. These extensions, together with streamlining the wing-to-fuselage fairing, have given the 747 more efficient performance at higher altitudes and for the longer ranges that it normally flies. When Boeing originally extended the upper fuselage for the series 300, they realized an improvement in fuel efficiency of about 12 percent. With the wing improvements of the series 400, an additional seven percent—for a total of about 25 percent—has been added to the efficiency of the original airframe. Of course, all of these improvements must be taken in the context of improvements in engine and engine nacelle designs. In addition, the series 400 wing—as

United Airlines

In addition to taking over the Pacific route structure, United took over a large number of Pan Am 747s after the buyout. This aircraft, N146UA, was originally registered N537PA and put into service by Pan Am on June 9, 1978.

well as the entire aircraft—makes better use of more sophisticated composite and lighter weight materials. All of the wing control surfaces are "fly by wire." Also, the series 400 has a much more advanced cockpit, discussed separately, and the horizontal tail can now be used to hold up to 330 gallons (1249 lt), of fuel, which gives the aircraft additional range.

There are 18 wheels on the 747, two for the nose gear and 16 main wheels. The reason for so many wheels is, of course, to reduce the overall loading at the runway, which is also called the *single wheel weight*. This allows the 747 to operate from most conventional airports that can handle wide-bodied aircraft. In this regard, the 747 is similar to an "average" aircraft. It is also somewhat "average" for its ground-handling characteristics, for which the steerable nosewheel is augmented by steerable main trucks. The main gear is mounted both in the wings and in the fuselage, and the fuselage-mounted set are steerable. On recent 747s, Boeing has used a white epoxy-type paint for corrosion control on the interior and wheel well areas.

Electronics

All of the 747's electronics are either dual or triple redundant. Curiously, while the more critical systems, such as the Inertial Navigation System (INS), are triple redundant, as the technology has advanced, one critical component has dropped from triple or quadruple redundant to double redundant. I'm referring to the flight crew, which has dwindled over the years from four to two, but not without much anguish. It is interesting to note that the early 747s contain, on average, about a million movable parts, about 135 miles of electrical wiring, and about a mile of hydraulics. With the advent of the new series 400, some of the wiring has been reduced (by about 30%), but the rest of the load stays about the same.

Although the particulars of the aircraft delivered are in accordance with the individual customer's specifications, the basics are easy to discuss. Basic communications on the 747

Also an early user of the 747, this series 100, with the bright red tail and cheat line and the white maple leaf, was put into service by Air Canada in February of 1971. It illustrates the later style Pratt and Whitney engines.

With the vertical wingtip winglets and extended upper fuselage, the series 400 is pretty easily recognized. In Northwest service from the beginning, this series 400 now sports a new paint job to go with the recent Pratt and Whitney PW4000 engines.

include standard dual Very High Frequency (VHF) and High Frequency (HF) systems. In normal use, the VHF is used for local airport and Air Traffic Control (ATC) communications, while the HF is used for longer range communications. The aircraft are also provided with a variety of inflight entertainment, public address, and lighting systems. Typically, a combination of two radio altimeters and weather radars are provided to ensure sky location. For earth location, as already discussed, the aircraft is usually provided with triple Inertial Navagation Systems. There are usually three each of the Visible Landing System/Instrument Landing System (VLS/ILS) navigation and two each of the various Automatic Direction Finder (ADF) and marker beacon systems used for landing in modern and primitive airports.

The 747 is equipped with the latest in stall warning systems, central data management and warning systems, central instrument warning systems, and ground proximity warning systems. Of course, full automatic pilots and navigation systems are available. The 747 can be fully certified for both Category II and Category III landings. Swissair 747s, for example, are certified for Category IIIA landings, where the decision height is 19.7 feet (6 m) and the horizontal visibility is 492 feet (150 m). Other carriers fly the aircraft with different certifications, depending on requirements.

Of course, the aircraft is equipped with a "black box." Actually, the black box is not black at all; it is Day-Glo orange, orange-red, or even bright yellow with contrasting stripes. Also, it should not be called *a* box, but rather *boxes*. There are two components to each "black box," and some larger airliners carry an additional pair of each. The components are the Flight Data Recorder (FDR) and the Cockpit Voice Recorder (CVR). The 747 is equipped with the latest version of each. The FDR is used to record the flight characteristics of the aircraft during the flight, while the CVR records the last half hour or so of the cockpit conversation. The device records conversation inside the cockpit area as well as communications between the flight deck crewmembers and the ground. The most recent half hour is determined mechanically by the tape, since it is only a half hour long and automatically erases as it overwrites. The reason for a half-hour record is that when the requirement for the CVR was promulgated in 1966, it was noted that a crisis in the air rarely lasts more than half an hour. The FDR has been required by FAA regulations since 1957.

This Iran Air SP illustrates to good advantage the flexing of the outboard forward wing flaps after they have been extended. Against the lower wing surface, they are flat. As they are extended, their surfaces curve, a flexing property of the honeycomb.

This photo shows to good advantage the forward cargo door, which is being used on this Swissair series 300 in Zurich to load cargo, as opposed to the passenger baggage normally put in this compartment. As can be seen, the cargo doors are not plug-type doors and require a secure locking mechanism.

As the Boeing has aged, these instruments have been updated to meet either the latest in safety requirements or the latest in technology, as the customer order dictates. While this has been particularly true of safety warning and management systems, nowhere has it been more obvious than with the instrument cluster. From the original 747 up through the series 300, an analog flight deck was used. For an analog flight deck (also called a "clockwork" flight deck), which is the traditional method of instrumenting an aircraft, each separate concern is connected to a separate sensor on one end and to a separate instrument on the other end. Thus, for example, an oil temperature gauge for a four-engine plane would have a thermal sensor in the oil for each engine individually connected to a separate oil gauge for each engine on the flight deck. Given the number of engine characteristics necessary to monitor and a four-engine aircraft, this can lead to a large number of instruments for a fairly short period of time. For fuel management and communications awareness, there are a similarly large number of gauges. Likewise, for the actual flight characteristics (including altitude and attitude, direction, and speed), there are separate instruments. Navigation requires its own instruments. By instrumenting the 747 in analog fashion, Boeing built an aircraft that required a three-man crew—one to manage the engine instruments (the flight engineer) and two to manage the aircraft, typically, one to manage the actual flying and one to do the rest of the work. During this time, the ordinary 747 had something like 800 instruments and switches for the crew to monitor.

By the time work began on the series 400, many advances had been made in cockpit instrumentation. This led to the so-called "glass" cockpit, wherein the major functions are displayed on a glass screen not unlike a TV screen. That single instrument can serve a variety of functions. It also allows for the incorporation of integrated monitoring and warning systems, wherein a specific function will be displayed either only periodically or

With delivery of the new series 400, Japan Airlines adopted a more subdued gray marking, although the bright red crane remains on the vertical tail. Also note the new General Electric engines used to power this aircraft.

only when there is something out-of-bounds for a set threshold. Additionally, it allows the individual user to go from dial-type to tape-type displays by simply programming the display driver and not by reinstrumenting the entire aircraft. By doing this, Boeing was able to reduce the number of instrument faces in the series 400 cockpit to around 300, which can be managed by a crew of two. A natural fallout of this type of digital instrumentation has been improvements in the maintenance and on-line diagnostics capabilities of the system to aid the maintenance crew in fixing problems.

Improvements in the Flight Management System (FMC) have also been possible. The series 400 system is much faster and more responsive, and covers a large variety of problems and criteria. Although response times as little as 1/7 of those of previous 747 technology aircraft have been realized (largely because of the integration of such functions as throttle control, which previously was managed by a separate system), the jury is still out on this level of automation.

The entire integrated package, as seen from the cockpit seat on the instrument panel, is called the Electronic Flight Instrument System (EFIS). First presented operationally to the airline community on the Airbus A300 series (notably, the A320), these have rapidly found a permanent place in the cockpit. Among other things, they make it much easier for the pilots to learn the new system, and to migrate from one type of aircraft cockpit to another. The basic format is six Cathode Ray Tubes (CRTs), or TV screens. These are arranged on the instrument panel, two directly in front of each pilot and two between each pilot. The screens directly in front of each pilot provide for the primary flight stability and location, or navigation information, and are identical in each pair. The two shared provide the engine information.

Singapore 747 shows to good advantage the new Pratt and Whitney PW4000 engines and pylons, as originally delivered with the series 400.

With the new Swissair markings of red tail, white cross, and dark brown and black lower fuselage with a white crown, this red-lettered Swissair series 300 shows to good advantage the SUD (Stretched Upper Deck).

Boeing put its own stamp on this type of design by offering much larger screens and more fully integrated systems. The four basic displays that can be brought up on any of the six big screens in the 747 cockpit are flight, navigation (including radar), engine, and systems. Typically, as on the Airbus, the shared displays are used for engine above and systems below, and the displays directly in front of the pilots for flight, on the right, and navigation on the left. Of particular interest on the flight display is the heading, which is displayed at the bottom portion of the screen as an arc, rather than the more traditional number. One instrument shows the Primary Flight Display (PFD), and together with airspeed, the primary information shown on it is called the Electronic Attitude Director Indicator (EADI). The other, a navigation display, is called the Electronic Horizontal Situation Indicator (EHSI). It offers a "look behind" capability, as well as integration of weather radar with flight plans and approaches. Typically, these displays are used with the PFD to the outside of the aircraft and the navigation display to the center. The two center displays are the Engine Indication and Crew Alerting System (EICAS). These displays are shared, without change, with the 757/767 cockpit environment. Standard is the vertical tape display, although the round dial display is also available. The lower of the displays provides information about the engines, including compressor speeds, oil pressures and temperatures, and engine thrust ratios. The upper display is for the rest of the aircraft systems, including the door positions and the hydraulic pressures and fuel states. On newer aircraft, tire pressure is also shown on this display.

Other improvements in the new series 400 over previous 747s have been in the carbon brakes, digital electronics used to control the engines from an integrated flight management system, fuel in the tailplane for longer range, greater travel for the vertical rudder, and plumbing in both the upper and lower decks for up to 26 lavatories. There are also several crew rest and bunk options offered, from bunks just aft of the flight deck to a crew rest area all the way at the rear of the extended upper cabin.

As with many carriers, Qantas adopted new livery with the advent of their Rolls Royce-engined series 400 aircraft. In this case, the kangaroo is preserved on the tail, but the overall impact is to increase the contrast between the white fuselage and the red tail, with understated Queens and Northern Territories Air Service (QANTAS) logos on the fuselage.

Known as the ''clockwork'' cockpit, this early series 747 three-man cockpit has approximately 690 dials and lights to monitor and 280 switches, compared to the 300 indicators and 200 switches found in the base-line 747 two-man cockpit.

33

The newer wings are of the same basic 747 design, with the improvements discussed above, but are made of much improved composites, which reduce the weight of the wing by about 5000 pounds. One final interesting advancement in the 747 has been in the overhead bins. While the cost of handling baggage has continued to rise, largely because of unions, only in the last few years have carriers begun to realize the advantages to letting the passengers carry their own baggage. There is more than enough incentive for this, and one might even be able to build a convincing argument that the carriers *deliberately* reduce the number of people handling baggage so that it takes an unbearable time to collect one's bags! To accommodate carry-on luggage in the 747, Boeing engineers have remodeled the hinging and location of the overhead bins, resulting in an increase in the volume from the previous 4.4 cubic feet to 10.6 cubic feet, although the new bins are provided in 60-inch segments.

More passengers (particularly in the upper cabin area) naturally means more passenger ammenities, including gallies and rest rooms. This has led to a new rest room in the upper deck, which is somewhat larger and comes complete with a window!

Production Problems

As the series 400 went into production, Boeing was beset with a number of problems. Boeing was determined to certify the new series aircraft for all three types of engines at virtually the same time. This, combined with the increased electronic sophistication of the new 747, led to production problems. Although both Boeing and the FAA were working overtime to achieve the proper certifications, there were inevitable delays. Many of the delays were due to the fact that although the new aircraft was being certified as a variant of the old aircraft (that is, the series 400 was a variant of the series 300), there were significant differences. The series 300 was different from the series 200 primarily due to the extension of the upper fuselage. The series 400 retained the basic fuselage configuration of the series 300, but in addition to the changes in the wings, could carry fuel internally in the horizontal tail and had an all-electronic, two-man cockpit compared to the series 300's three-man cockpit. This change involved as many as 40,000 wires being terminated differently in the new aircraft—a problem of some magnitude.

This Alitalia aircraft, in addition to showing the all-cargo version with no cabin windows, also illustrates to good advantage the early style General Electric engines.

To add more problems, some Boeing employees went on strike during the preliminary production of the aircraft. Although Boeing was not at penalty for delays in delivery due to strikes for most of their series 400 customers, they were liable for other delays, and were required to negotiate penalties. At the same time, several carriers were experiencing problems with their flight crews, who were uncertain about the two-man cockpit. In early days, trains had engineers, who worked the controls, and firemen, who shoveled coal or wood for the steam. With the advent of the diesel locomotive, the use of the fireman was unclear. But, after long and painful negotiations, firemen continued to work the new locomotives. In somewhat the same manner, flight deck crews, while applauding new digital avionics, were quick to point out that if a three-man crew each averages $100,000 per year, then a two-man crew, which has the same responsibility as the previous three-man crew, should average $150,000 each per year! 747 operators were quick to notice this reasoning and point out that the Direct Operating Cost (DOC) of the aircraft due to higher crew salaries can be as much as 16 percent of the total, including airport fees, fuel, cleaning, entertainment, and replenishing all of the consumables on board. For airline carriers, who paid more for the higher-technology two-man cockpit, this has been a thorny problem. Such negotiations, shrouded in the number of hours flown per two-week consecutive period and on even-numbered deployment days, are difficult for the average fare-paying passenger to understand. It is not an easy problem. On the one hand, the pilots are quick to point out their tremendous responsibility during individual decisions; but on the other, whenever there is a problem with the aircraft, pilot organizations are quick to spread the blame to as many air traffic controllers and ground handlers as they can reasonably include, through their rather formidable unions. In addition, there is no clear evidence that automation of the cockpit makes the skies any safer, and many pilots are concerned about the loss of basic airmanship skills, such as flying the aircraft.

David H. Minton

On landing approach, this standard Pratt and Whitney-powered Northwest 747 shows to good advantage the triple slotted trailing edge flaps.

Docking in Honolulu, this series 300 shows the variety of ground handling equipment associated with loading and replenishing one of Singapore Airlines' Pratt and Whitney-powered "Bigtops."

This Qantas SP, docking in Honolulu, shows to good advantage the early Rolls Royce engines used on the Boeing series 100/200/300 aircraft.

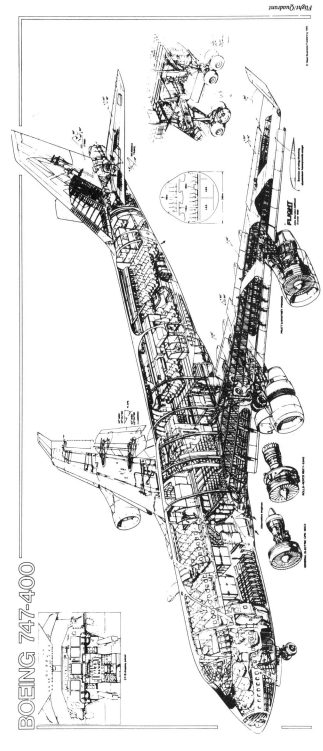

BOEING 747-400

Flight/Quadrant

This drawing shows both the advanced 21st century technology Electronic Flight Instrument System (EFIS) instrument panel and each of the three engines available for the series 400 aircraft, as well as many other important details.

The Future

Future versions of the 747, outside of the currently produced series 400, are still on the drawing board. However, several ideas remain constant throughout the development of the aircraft, including extension of the upper cabin to carry more passengers and improvements in the cockpit management system, including reductions in the flight deck loading. Eventual re-engining of the aircraft, or development of a new version based on the newer technology engines now being developed (Pratt and Whitney PW4000, General Electric GE90, Rolls Royce Trent) is inevitable. We know that it is just a matter of time until the new engines go to 70,000 pounds of static thrust and beyond. Therefore, a 700-passenger very long range 747 is certainly not out of the question.

Further off yet, there has been discussion of a 1000-passenger 747. Boeing is in a curious position in this regard. On the one hand, there is no other company currently capable of producing an aircraft that can compete with the 747 in terms of passenger loading and range, but on the other hand, Boeing is easily able to compete with itself. This is especially difficult because orders for the aircraft are so deeply backlogged and the ideas for improvement quickly roll off the technology assembly line. Boeing must exercise care not to compete with themselves faster than they can produce aircraft, but at the same time they must be sure to provide all of the necessary support for existing aircraft to survive a long time.

Certainly, one of the most interesting 747 proposals has been extension of the aircraft by about 20 feet forward of the wing, including the upper cabin, and about 25 feet aft of the wing, using the ultra-high-bypass engines discussed above. Alternatives include discussions of a full double-decker aircraft, something like the old Stratoliner. Finally, the 747, both old and new versions, continues to increase in range and capability, still setting records.

It has always been the case that customers could change one of their orders or options for an earlier aircraft. Thus, for example, if a carrier ordered options on a series 300, they could elect to convert this aircraft, upon execution of the order, to a series 200F. Recently, however, there has been a new trend, where the carrier may take options on aircraft yet to be specified. This trend, combined with the possible new aircraft posed on the horizon, ensures us of many interesting variations of the 747 yet to be built.

4

In Uniform

T HE BOEING 747 has appeared in uniform in a number of interesting and somewhat unusual ways. In addition to service with the United States Air Force (USAF), it has also flown for the Iranian Air Force (IAF) and the National Aeronautics and Space Administration (NASA), and has served as the personal transport of the Imperial Saudi family. Two 747s have been outfitted as Air Force One, the United States Presidential aircraft.

United States Air Force

Two versions of the Boeing E-4 aircraft have been made, the E-4A and the E-4B. On 23 February 1973, Electronic Systems Division (ESD) of the USAF announced that it would use two 747 series 200 aircraft, which were to be outfitted as Airborne Command Posts. These 747 versions would replace the existing EC-135 Airborne Command Posts, based on the Boeing 707 platform. The plan was to outfit the two 747 aircraft with the original, but updated, EC-135 equipment. These interim aircraft would be known as E-4As. Both of these aircraft were powered by the original Pratt and Whitney engines, with integrated avionics installed on the airframe by E-Systems.

Later, as new avionics became available and integrated into the system capability of the aircraft, two new 747s would be delivered and the original E-4As would be retrofitted to E-4B status. Eventually, all four aircraft would be fitted with the newer General Electric F103-GE-100 turbofans, and these 747s are known as E-4Bs.

Originally based at Andrews Air Force Base, just outside of Washington, D.C., under the dual command of both the National Military Command System and the Strategic Air Command (SAC), the E-4's mission has since been placed solely under SAC. As a result, the aircraft are now based at Offett Air Force Base in Nebraska. Until recently, these airborne command posts have been kept aloft 24 hours a day. With the recent thaw in the cold war, the aircraft are no longer flown 24 hours a day, but on a random and intermittent basis.

The main deck of the E-4 is divided into six major functional areas, with the corresponding mission equipment for each area housed appropriately. These major functions include the National Command Authorities (NCA) work area, a conference area, a briefing room, a battle staff work area, a communications control center, and a crew rest area. Below the main deck is housed a technical control capability for the on-board communications and a small but complete maintenance capability. The upper flight deck houses, of course, the cockpit area. In addition, the rear portion accommodates a navigation station and a flight crew rest area. The E-4 is, of course, capable of refueling in flight.

Iranian Air Force

It has been said that the Shah of Iran read *Aviation Week* instead of *Playboy*. Whether or not this is true, it is certain that during the Nixon administration, with the help of Henry Kissinger, the Shah pursued an aggressive policy of outfitting his nation with new and modern high-technology aircraft. As a result, the Imperial Iranian Air Force is the only other national air force that has had the benefit of the great range and incredible cargo-carrying capability of the Boeing 747.

Although all of the missions of the Iranian 747s are, of course, not fully known, it is certain that the fleet usually carried inflight refueling capability and was often used to

Seen here at Amsterdam in Imperial Iranian Air Force markings, this 747 shows an in-flight refueling capability. This aircraft is overall silver and gray, with a dark blue cheatline and black titles with the three colored national insignia and flash on the vertical tail.

After the fall of the Shah of Iran, the markings of the military aircraft were changed from those of the Imperial Iranian Air Force to those of the Iranian Air Force. Except for the change in the initials and the addition of Farsi script, the basic colors of the aircraft remained the same, white fuselage with dark blue markings and the Iranian green/white/red fin flash on the tail.

Although not truly a military uniform, "The Odd Couple" performed the duty for NASA of shuttling the shuttle from landing site to launch site.

transport both troops and cargo, as well as the royal family. After the fall of the monarchy, these 747s remained on the inventory for a while as Iranian Air Force aircraft, generally being used in the same capacity; the refueling capability was removed from at least some of them. Eventually these 747s were transferred to Iran Air, where at least some of them continue to serve.

NASA

Before they ever flew, NASA discovered that it would have to solve a unique problem with its orbiter (Space Shuttle) fleet. The orbiters were going to land at Edwards Air Force

Base, in California, but be launched by a booster from Cape Kennedy (Canaveral) in Florida. Therefore, they would have to be moved from one place to the other by some simple means. Although briefly considered, building a break-apart shuttle was never seen as a realistic solution to this problem. Consequently, NASA took a 747-123 aircraft (which was being used for heavy, wide-bodied aircraft vortex flow research) and created what would come to be known as "The Odd Couple." (Actually, it was really known as NASA 905, but it was usually called "The Odd Couple," probably because of a popular television series of the time.)

NASA Dryden Flight Research center built a so-called mate/demate apparatus, which was used to mount and dismount the shuttle from the 747 during the test phase. Boeing performed the necessary modifications to the aircraft, which included mounting the NASA-designed "piggyback" frame on the aircraft fuselage, strengthening the fuselage, instrumenting the link-up capabilities, rearranging the horizontal tail assembly to include the new vertical surfaces on the outboard edges, and much of the flight testing and certification.

The first mated flight was completed on 18 February 1977, with the so-called SCA (Shuttle Carrier Aircraft) lifting the orbiter *Enterprise* at a takeoff weight of 584,000 pounds (264,890 kg). In this configuration, landings are generally made without the use of thrust reversers, or with minimum use of thrust reversers, to minimize damage to the orbiter. Later, on 13 August of the same year, at Edwards Air Force Base, the first free-fall launch of the orbiter from the mother craft was accomplished from an altitude of approximately 22,800 feet.

Originally, NASA planned to have two 747s modified to this configuration, but with setbacks in the space program (caused, in part, by the *Challenger* disaster), the delivery of

Boeing Military Airplanes

Seen on liftoff for its maiden flight, the new VC-25 will become Air Force One when the President of the United States is aboard. It is covered with a protective coat of green paint in this photo, repainted as Air Force One prior to delivery.

the second aircraft was delayed. Finally, in 1988, the second NASA 747 became fully operational. These two aircraft, remain the only way to transport the fully assembled orbiter from the landing site to the launch site after a shuttle mission.

Air Force One

From the early days of air travel, a special transport for the President of the United States has been used. One of the first of these was a DC-4 called the *Sacred Cow*, particularly when the President was aboard. The first jet aircraft to become the President's personal transport was a Boeing 707-320 series, which carried the military designation of VC-135. It came to be called Air Force One when the President is aboard. During the Reagan years, it was determined that the venerable VC-135 Air Force One would have to be replaced. For almost three decades, Air Force One had been based on the Boeing 707-320C platform in a VIP (Very Important Person) configuration. Although various airframes have rotated through Andrews Air Force Base at different times, the basic aircraft remained the same since it was first put into service on October 12, 1962.

In addition to all of the complicated communications and military equipment added to the VC-25, the entire fuselage area had to be changed to suit the mission; air stairs and in-flight refueling were added.

Eventually the USAF decided on two series 200 747s as replacements; these will be known as VC-25s. These two aircraft are fitted with the General Electric CF6-80C2B1 engines and both have in-flight refueling capabilities. The new aircraft will easily accommodate a crew of 23 and a passenger load of 70, which is nearly twice the payload of the VC-135, although the crew size is somewhat increased. This is, in large part, due to the increased mission capability of the aircraft. Inside, the VC-25 includes a presidental suite (with office, stateroom, and lavatory), conference rooms, emergency medical capability, and rest areas for the president's staff. There is also an area for the news media, and two galleys. The upper deck accommodates the Air Force crew, who fly and maintain the aircraft, as well as the medical and communications capabilities. The lower portion of the aircraft, normally used for passenger baggage, on the VC-25 provides the air stairs, automated self-contained cargo loaders, spare parts, extra meals, and specific mission-related equipment.

Insofar as possible, the aircraft provides full-up on-board communications, including associated cryptographic equipment, and all associated computers, telephones, faxes, and radios. All of the communications are handled by a combination of Rockwell Collins and E-Systems equipment. Shielding from electromagnetic pulses (EMP), as would be generated by high-altitude nuclear denotations, as well as conventional electromagnetic interference/electromagnetic shielding (EMI/EMS) are provided. In addition to the problems associated with the delivery of an aircraft carrying almost twice as much wire as a standard series 200, tests of the new cabin cargo doors will have to be completed, as well as full-up testing of all of the on-board communications capability.

The first VC-25 rolled out in September, 1989, and was successfully flown 26 January 1990, then placed in service in late 1990.

Other Uniforms

In addition to use as a VIP transport for the government of Saudi Arabia, several 747s have been outfitted to support what is known as the U.S. CRAF (Civil Reserve Air Fleet). After modification, these aircraft are then called C-19A when used in military service. These modifications involved 19 Pan American 747 series 100 aircraft, which were converted to make the jets more capable of carrying both troops and cargo in the event of a national emergency. In addition to the conversion directly related to the CRAF program, Pan Am completed approximately $2 million in work on each of these aircraft as well.

The basic modifications included a strengthened floor, which involved replacement of the floor beams, and the addition of a new 10-foot-high cargo door on the left side of the aircraft, aft of the wings. In addition, improved cargo-handling capabilities were added to each aircraft. These modifications were accomplished by stripping the passenger interiors out of the Pan Am aircraft, completing the modifications, and then reinstalling the interiors and returning the aircraft to passenger service. In the event of a national emergency, each of these aircraft could be pressed into service as either cargo or cargo/troop carriers in about 48 hours. A total of 19 aircraft have been so modified, of which 18 are still in operation, one having been lost over Lockerbie, Scotland, in 1988.

5

In the News

B ECAUSE of its size and capabilities, the Boeing 747 has been in the news almost since its very beginning. Newsworthy 747 events include record-setting time and distance flights, but as the 747 appeared in more and more of the world's fleets, other types of news events also occurred.

Due to the natural affinity of terrorists for news-grabbing possibilities using airliners and airliner communications, it is not surprising the 747 has been the target of some of the most tragic terrorist events in our time. And due to the very nature of aviation, airliners will be involved in accidents. Because the 747 is the largest commercial aircraft in the free world and it operates throughout the world, it is no surprise that it appears frequently in the news. Because of its enormous size, an accident involving a 747 can cause as many fatalities as several smaller airliners, so the sheer numbers of 747 fatalities can seem, at first glance, to be quite alarming.

The first production 747 to be put into service, N733PA, made the news when christened *Clipper Young America* on 12 December 1969 by Mrs. Pat Nixon. It was supposed to be put into service by Christmas. Instead, it made the news again when it missed its inaugural flight from New York to London on 21 January 1970. In the wee morning hours of 22 January 1970, N736PA, *Clipper Victor*, after being temporarily renamed *Clipper Young America*, was substituted and made the flight. Engine troubles had crippled the original *Clipper Young America*.

This aircraft, one of the first delivered to Pan Am, was originally equipped with Pratt and Whitney JT9D-1Bs, which were not the most reliable P&W engines. Subsequently, when the JT9D-3As became available, this aircraft (along with the rest of the Pan Am fleet) was re-engined and experienced relatively few engine problems.

Later, *Clipper Victor* resumed its original name and went on to a terrible tragedy at Tenerife. The original *Clipper Young America* was renamed *Clipper Constitution*, while the original *Clipper Constitution*, N735PA, was at the same time renamed *Clipper Young America*.

Although a bit bumpy for a start, it was the beginning for what would become the world's most significant airliner. It was first put into service by the same carrier who originally put the Boeing 707—also christened by a President's wife—into international service.

Setting Records

Like the SR-71, the recently retired Lockheed Blackbird, nearly every time the Boeing 747 does something different, it sets a new world record. The 747 is a record-size airliner. No other commercial aircraft can carry the numbers of people across the distances that are possible with the 747. Therefore, flights involving the 747 did, of their own merit, set numerous records.

Even before the first passenger-carrying flight discussed above, the very first flight of a 747, on 9 February 1969, is considered something of a milestone in the history of flight. After being put into commercial service, the 747 regularly made the news as new carriers introduced it on new routes. In addition, delivery flights to places such as South Africa and Australia commonly set records for time and distance. Flight times of 17 to 18 hours and distances of 10,200 miles became common. Delivery of a South African Airlines 747SP on 23-24 March 1976 required just such a record-setting flight. But aside from this sort of "bookkeeping" record-setting, the 747 was involved in even more interesting flights.

Flights around the world, while not exactly commonplace, became possible. These flights were available to revenue passengers. Flying a Pan American 747SP, Capt. Walter H. Mullikin set a round-the-world speed record on 1-3 May 1976. For this flight, Mullikin circumnavigated the globe, flying west to east, in about 46 hours, for an average speed record of 502 mph. On 28–31 October 1970, the same pilot, again flying a Pan Am 747SP, circumnavigated the globe via the North and South Poles. This trip covered a distance of 26,382 miles in a time of approximately 54 hours. In January of 1988, a United Airlines 747SP (previously owned by Pan Am) reduced this around-the-world record to less than 40 hours, with just two enroute stops in Athens and Taipei. As recently as 13 February 1990, a Pan American aircraft with Capt. William Frisbee set a new world speed record for a four-engine, non-SST airliner. Carrying 227 passengers and 17 crewmembers, Frisbee flew from Los Angeles to New York, a distance of 2461 miles, in a record setting 3 hours and 45 minutes—nothing like the SR-71, but pretty fast for an airliner.

Still in the news as the series 400 with its great range and capacity, goes into production and delivery, nearly every delivery flight to some distant location in Africa or Australia will produce a record-setting flight.

Several 747 (or models of 747s) have been in the movies. Thanks to great special effects, in the most recent a model of a 747 was destroyed in the movie *Die Hard II*. Other 747s have appeared in movies, as well. Three of the most famous are N9675, of American Airlines, which was featured in *Airport 75*; N9667, also of American Airlines, which made its debut painted as Stevens Corporation for *Airport 77*; and F-BPVA, which appeared in *La Bonne Annee*.

*Pan Am aircraft, such as this SP **Clipper Constitution,** have been in the news for a variety of record-setting flights, including around-the-world flights both over the poles and at the equator.*

Occasionally a 747 will figure in a catastrophic event. As we will see, with very few exceptions, problems experienced by 747s are usually caused by human actions—either the deliberate destruction of terrorism or mistakes. It should be noted that because of the relative availability of information concerning British and American events, the discussion that follows might seem to be biased against the United States and England. In reality, nothing is further from the truth, but information involving other foreign aircraft, particularly those from Middle East countries, is often not available. Because of this, not all of the incidents can be discussed in equal detail. In all, there have been 17 hulls destroyed since the first 747 was built. TABLE 5-1 lists, in chronological order, the major events involving the loss or significant destruction of a Boeing 747 that have so far been identified.

Crashes and Smashes

The first fatal accident involving a 747 happened to a Lufthansa aircraft on a flight out of Nairobi. On 20 November 1974, the plane was bound for Johannesburg, South Africa, on a flight from Frankfurt, West Germany. According to witnesses, the plane took off in a more-or-less normal fashion and then stalled and fell to the ground. There were 157 persons on board; of these, 59 died and 98 survived. This crash was attributed to an incorrect flap setting for takeoff, although the aircraft commander, Capt. Krack, testified he believed that the flaps were properly set. The actual takeoff was witnessed by a Sabena pilot, who testified that he noted not all of the training edge flaps appeared to be in the proper configuration.

The next major incident (not counting terrorism, addressed separately in the next section) involved an Air India aircraft on departure out of Calcutta, India. This 747 crashed

Table 5-1. Major incidents involving 747 aircraft.

Date	Aircraft	Carrier	Location	Incident
9/6/70	N738PA	Pan American	Cairo	Terrorist bombing, on the ground after hijacking.
7/23/72	JA8109	Japan Air Lines	Benghazi	Hijacked, blown up.
11/20/74	D-ABYB	Lufthansa	Nairobi	Crashed on takeoff; ruled pilot error.
6/12/75	N28888	Air France	Bombay	Taxi wheel well fire, repaired.
5/9/76	5-8104	IIAF	Madrid	Crashed on takeoff.
3/27/77	N736PA	Pan American	Tenerife	Hit by PH-BUF.
3/27/77	PH-BUF	KLM	Tenerife	Flew into N736PA.
1/1/78	VT-EBD	Air India	Bombay	Crashed on takeoff; ruled pilot error.
6/30/78	VT-EFO	Air India	Atlantic Ocean	Inflight explosion.
12/27/79	N771PA	Pan American	London	No. 4 pylon separated on landing, fire; blamed on previous collision with baggage truck.
1980	EP-ICC	Iran Air	Iran	Presumed.
11/18/80	HL-7445	KAL	Seoul	Crashed; suspect pilot error.
9/1/83	HL-7442	KAL	Sakalin	Missile attack.
10/18/83	N738PA	Pan American	Karachi	Crashed.
11/27/83	HK-2910	Avianca	Madrid	Crashed landing; suspect pilot error.
3/16/85	F-GDUA	UTA	Paris	Crashed.
8/12/85	JA8119	JAL	Tokyo	Came apart inflight; improper repair.
11/28/87	ZS-SAR	SAA	Maritus	Smoke reported; crashed landing.
12/21/88	N739PA	PAA	Lockerbie	Inflight explosion.
2/19/89	unk	Flying Tigers	Singapore	Crashed landing; suspect crew error.
2/24/80	N4713U	UAL	Honolulu	Came apart inflight; cargo door failure.

into the Bay of Bombay. This incident was interesting for several reasons. For one, the pilot literally flew the aircraft into the bay immediately after takeoff. The incident occurred on New Year's Day, 1978. During the investigation, the pilot, who survived, testified that the attitude inclination indicator had misled him into overcompensating. Indeed he did overcompensate, because the aircraft was nearly inverted when it hit the water. The CVR (Cockpit Voice Recorder) did show that the copilot tried to dispute the pilot's decision. The copilot based his decision on a variety of other instruments available and the fact that it was a relatively clear morning and the true horizon was readily visible, but the captain elected to disregard all of this evidence and flew his aircraft into the bay; 219 people on board, passengers and crew, perished. The presiding Indian judge ruled that the Captain had been drinking at a New Year's Eve party the night before, and alcohol, combined with high blood pressure medication, caused him to lose orientation. This, combined with a *possible* misfunction of a *single* instrument on the aircraft, caused the crash.

There were several accidents which followed, typically attributed to some combination of human error. These included the Avianca crash in Madrid, the KAL incident in Seoul (for which the flight crew was arrested), and others. In several of these cases, the aircraft were on cargo operations and no passenger fatalities were incurred. A recent example would be the crash of a Flying Tigers 747 on approach to Singapore on 19 February 1989. The crew of four on board perished. It is thought that because this airport uses two separate radio approaches, the crew might have become confused. In any event, they crashed the aircraft into high ground several miles from the runway.

Along with a Pan Am 747, a KLM 747 similar to the one shown here was involved in one of the most serious aviation accidents yet recorded—at Tenerife.

Tenerife

The most serious aircraft accident in history, in terms of fatalities, occurred at Tenerife, in Spain's Canary Islands. A collision involving two aircraft, particularly when that collision occurs on the ground, is not as rare as one might hope. Incidents involving 747 and some other aircraft or ground equipment are relatively frequent, up to one or two a year; collisions involving two 747s are thankfully infrequent. As recently as 20 June 1988, at Vienna International Airport, a South African Airlines 747 collided with a Royal Jordanian 747. The subsequent damage to both aircraft was substantial, particularly the nose of the Royal Jordanian airliner. "Near incidents," such as the reported "almost" collision between a British 747 and an El Al 747 just south of Iceland in 1988, are also relatively common. At Tenerife, however, everything went wrong at once.

Tenerife is the largest (although not the grandest) of Spain's Canary Islands. On this particular Sunday, 27 March 1977, it was foggy and busier than usual. There had been a terrorist bombing at Los Rodeos Airport, on Grand Canary Island. A terrorist bomb detonated at the airport check-in counter and had temporarily closed the airport. Aircraft enroute were diverted to Las Palmas, on Tenerife. Two such aircraft were a Pan Am 747 and a KLM 747. The Pan Am aircraft was a charter flight, carrying mostly retired people, bound from Los Angeles, California, to Los Rodeos. There, the passengers expected to meet up with a luxury cruise ship for a tour of the Mediterranean. The Pan Am aircraft had stopped enroute in New York to pick up additional passengers. The KLM flight had originated at Amsterdam. It was full of mostly younger people, bound for a resort hotel in Los Rodeos.

Both aircraft had landed. The KLM captain, in the interest of saving time, had elected to refuel as he waited for departure to Los Rodeos, where he would normally have refueled. Because his aircraft blocked the Pan Am aircraft, after Los Rodeos reopened, both planes had to wait until KLM refueled. KLM was then number one for departure, PAA number two.

For reasons we will never fully grasp, the KLM pilot released brakes and began to take off without completed clearance. This is not easy to understand, because the pilot was one of KLM's most experienced. The tower, enshrouded in the fog, could not see what was happening on the runway, nor did it have local radar to help locate aircraft. Because of the large number of aircraft diverted from Las Palmas, there was congestion on the taxiway. It was therefore necessary for the Pan Am aircraft to taxi partly on the active runway, as had the KLM aircraft before it, to arrive at the takeoff point behind KLM. For Pan Am, this involved going about halfway down the active runway and then moving to the adjacent taxi strip. At the far end of the airport, the takeoff point location, the taxi strip was uncongested. There, it would have waited for the KLM aircraft to clear, and then made its own takeoff. Unfortunately, it was still on the active runway when the KLM aircraft began its takeoff roll.

Although much has been made of the fact that it was supposed to exit at ramp 3 and instead continued to ramp 4, which caused it to be on the active runway longer than it otherwise might, this truly occludes the problem. The real problem occurred because of inadequate communications between the KLM crew and the tower. It has been suggested that Capt. van Zanten, concerned with crew service times, either neglected or overlooked proper departure verification. For a pilot of his experience, this is extremely unlikely. It is almost certain that Capt. van Zanten, on the KLM aircraft, simply misunderstood his clearance.

Because the accident occurred in contained space, tapes and records were available. We know a lot about it. We know that Capt. Gibbs, on the Pan Am aircraft, saw the KLM aircraft about 9.5 seconds before impact. At this time the KLM aircraft was moving about 145 mph. We believe it might have been two or three seconds later when Cap. van Zanten realized that the Pan Am aircraft was in his path. Capt. Gibbs had already initiated evasive action to his left. Capt. van Zanten continued to accelerate. We now believe he realized he was going to lose his own aircraft and was attempting to save the Pan Am jet. At the appropriate time, he pitched up and tried to hop over the Pan Am aircraft. Experts estimate he needed as little as an additional 15 feet. He did not have them, and his left main gear came in contact with the top of the Pan Am aircraft, just aft of the upper deck. Fuel and fire followed everywhere. All aboard the KLM aircraft perished; 61 survived from Pan Am aircraft, mostly from the right side, away from the collision. In all, 583 fatalities resulted from this crash, including those who later died from burns.

The PAA aircraft was the same *Clipper Victor* that had started it all, departing from New York Kennedy seven years earlier.

Terrorism

Acts of terrorism involving the 747—by comparison, probably no more dramatic or frequent than those involving other aircraft—still have the ability to grab the news like no other aircraft event. Because of the onboard communications, any hijacking will put the hijacker(s) immediately in the spotlight. Often, the purpose of the hijacking is little more than the opportunity to make a message known, which requires only communication. But more recently, the purpose is often significantly more sinister.

The bombing of an inflight aircraft is not an unusual event. Several known or suspected incidents can be traced back to the early 1950s, when such an event might occur in

Dennis Cross

Air India aircraft, with their very decorative markings, have been involved in serious incidents including a bombing over the north Atlantic and a crash in the Bay of Bombay.

order to collect on life insurance. On 20 February 1970, the pilot of a Swissair Convair 990, HB-ICD, reported a cargo compartment explosion on takeoff from Zurich. Shortly thereafter, possibly while attempting to land, the aircraft crashed. All 44 passengers and crew, enroute to Tel Aviv, died. An Arab political action group, which had been formed along with many others after the humiliating Arab defeat in the Six Day War, emphatically announced the destruction of this aircraft their first international operation. With this action, the PLFP (Popular Front for the Liberation of Palestine) rocketed to the front page of the world's awareness. Although yet to be involved in a 747 incident, this group was later to achieve fame in May 1972 Lod Airport massacre. After Swissair, many airliners carrying passengers were—and continue to be—bombed.

No bomb incidents involved the 747 until 30 June 1978. On that date, an Air India 747, VT-EFO, bound from Toronto to New Delhi with enroute stops in Montreal and London, disappeared over the north Atlantic somewhere near the coast of Ireland. More recently, however, the bombing of Pan Am flight 103 over Lockerbie, Scotland, captured the world's attention. Prior to these events, however, there was one other terrorist action involving the 747. This action resulted in the deliberate, complete, and total destruction of a 747 hull. This first terrorist incident involved Pan American N752PA, which was hijacked, along with three other aircraft, in a coordinated effort. On 6 September 1970, Pan American flight 93, outbound from Amsterdam to New York, was hijacked. Two students hijacked it, originally to Lebanon, but eventually to Cairo. This was early in the terrorist hijackings and, after negotiations, the hijackers were freed. The aircraft was blown up and destroyed. There were no fatalities. In that same incident, a TWA 707, an El Al 707, and a Swissair DC-8 were also hijacked. A security guard recognized that there was a problem with the El Al passengers. As a result, one of the hijackers was captured and another killed and the El Al attempt was aborted. The other three aircraft (TWA N8715T, Swissair HB-IDD, and Pan Am N752PA) were all taken. Subsequently, on 9 September 1970, a BOAC VC-10, G-ASGN, was also hijacked. The announced reason for the VC-10 hijacking was to free the terrorist captured during the aborted El Al attempt on 6 September. The Pan Am aircraft was destroyed by explosion immediately on arrival in Cairo on 6 September 1970. There were no negotiations concerning the remaining aircraft, all of the passengers were freed without harm, and these aircraft were subsequently destroyed by explosion in Jordan, at El Khana, on 13 September 1970. The organization that took credit for all of this destruction again identified itself as the Popular Front for the Liberation of Palestine (PLFP). This organization continued for several years as the scourge of civilization, in an on-again off-again relationship with the more accepted PLO (Palestinian Liberation Organization) and today still represents the ultimate mechanical conscience which lacks human spirit or purpose.

Much later, in Benghazi, under very different circumstances, JA8109 would meet a similar fate.

Lockerbie

After completion of analysis of the Air India crash, the Indian commission that investigated this event came up with a number of findings that could have had an advantageous impact on international airliner security. Although 329 persons on board the aircraft were destroyed in the incident, it did not capture the world's attention. In part, this is possibly due to the fact that it did not occur near Christmas. But one should recall that the wreckage was never recovered; hence dramatic photos in news magazines were not possible.

Among the findings of the commission were the now-recognized fact that it is very difficult to ensure the discovery of modern plastic explosives using X-ray and sniffer means. As a result, they recommended more exhaustive hand searches. Additionally, they found that the destruction of the aircraft was probably due to a bomb placed in the forward baggage compartment. On detonation, this bomb probably disabled the aircraft's electronics equipment, including the "black box."

The report loosely implicated factions active during the Tamil revolution, which was ongoing at the time. However, because the destruction occurred over the Atlantic, little of the wreckage was recovered. Some dedicated members of the commission remained "doubting Thomases," as it were, because they could not put their hands through the scars rent in the fuselage side by the explosion. For this reason, among others, the results of the report were not widely disseminated.

Although it is probably overly optimistic to imagine that the dissemination of this report could have had a positive effect on the Pan Am flight 103 tragedy, the similarities between the destruction of the two aircraft are noteworthy. This is particularly true with respect to the lack of communications from the aircraft after the explosion. Although it is believed that many of the passengers and crew remained conscious after the explosion, they were unable to communicate because of electronics equipment failures. Generally, on most passenger-carrying 747s, baggage is carried in the forward compartment and cargo in the rear. The electronics bay is located near the forward compartment. One of the findings from the Air India incident was a recommendation for relocation of this electronics equipment. But this finding was never widely distributed.

On the afternoon of 21 December 1988, Pan American flight 103 was leveling off after late departure from London Heathrow, outbound for New York. Aboard, all was fine. The pilots were probably just into their first cup of coffee when the bomb exploded. The bomb was in the forward hold, and the aircraft separated forward of the wing. There has been interesting discussion about the stability of the rear portion of the aircraft, but it is unlikely that the passengers and cabin crew in this portion of the aircraft had any real recognition of the problem. Certainly they knew they were out of control and going to crash. The noise and wind, coupled with the tumbling, would have made the rear compartments terrible. Passengers located between the sections as they were breaking up would have fallen from the plane. The rear section also separated into at least two major sections prior to impact.

In the forward portion, however, there would be another story. There would have been terrible noise and confusion, but there is little doubt that the flight deck crew would have been able to quickly determine that they were no longer flying an aircraft and could do nothing about it. The forward portion would have fallen like a rock. It is enticing to imagine that somehow it would have oriented itself in free-fall, but evidence from the wreckage makes it clear this did not happen. It landed on its side. There was no control and no orientation.

Parts of aircraft and humans, along with baggage and cargo, were thrown over an area of 1/2 mile wide and 2.5 miles long across the southern portion of the city of Lockerbie.

It is well-known that the citizens of Lockerbie, although 11 of their own were killed, opened their hearts and their arms to the survivors of relatives on Flight 103. In a remarkable display of courage and fortitude, the people of Lockerbie became a focus of strength for those who lost relatives and friends in the explosion. It has often been suggested Pan

Am and the Federal Aviation Agency (FAA) did not. Curiously, this should not be a surprise. Like any bureaucracy, in order to continue to survive, both Pan Am and the FAA depend in large part on the ability to ignore events beyond their control. Certainly, Flight 103 falls within this category. It was an event for which we were truly unprepared, even though we recognized clearly that it could happen—indeed had happened to other carriers. For this reason, neither the FAA nor the carrier were prepared to deal with the next of kin.

Although there is some controversy concerning the details of the actual bomb and how it was placed on the aircraft, we are relatively certain of some details. We are certain the bomb was made of Semtex, a Czechoslovakian-made plastic explosive. The explosive probably weighed about 2.5 pounds and was detonated in what is called a "Toshiba" type device. The name derives from the fact that the explosive, along with the detonator and battery, was housed in a portable radio of the type made by Toshiba, or other companies. (Toshiba has never been implicated in any way in this or other similar devices.) No final announcement has been made concerning the actual trigger device. Three typical types of trigger device are common for these types of bombs: an altitude-detonated device, a timer device, and a remote control device. Although any of these is possible, the timer device is most likely for two reasons. First, it is the simplest, consistent with the checked baggage theory. Second, the aircraft was late getting off at London; had it been on schedule, a timer device bomb would have exploded over the north Atlantic, not very far from the earlier Air India wreckage. Virtually none of the wreckage would have been recovered.

In all, 259 people aboard the aircraft suffered and died. Since the wreckage landed in the Scottish village of Lockerbie, there were an additional 11 casualties on the ground. One announced reason for the bombing was in retaliation for the Iranian Air incident, in which the USS *Vincennes* shot down an Iranian Airbus in a combat zone. However, no final or conclusive reason for the explosion has yet been provided.

The President's Commission on Aviation Security (also called the Lockerbie commission) made a number of recommendations. Several positive actions have resulted from this commission. The commission discovered that the FAA, like many bureaucracies, was process- rather than event-oriented, or "reactive" rather than "proactive." In the words of the commission findings, the FAA had something of a checklist mentality. Prior to the destruction of Pan Am Flight 103, FAA security bulletins rarely required specific action. Now, specific actions are frequently recommended. Transportation Secretary S. Skinner has also named Vice Admiral C. E. Robbins, USCG, as director to the newly established Office of Intelligence and Security. Additionally, security at all high-risk airports has been increased, as well as augmentation to the positive identification of the passenger baggage.

Even prior to the recommendations of the commission, the FAA had begun testing the Thermo Neutron Activation (TNA) type of devices at high risk airports. Although there is significant controversy about the effectiveness of this detector, it is known that a vapor detector, also called a "sniffer," and x-ray would probably not have been effective in detecting the Flight 103 device. Curiously, one of the most effective search methods, recommended long before the Flight 103 incident occurred, is increased hand searches. Unfortunately, these cost more money than automated methods, as well as taking longer. As technologies mature in the detector areas, we can expect to see new devices. Increases in manning at those international airports identified as "high risk" have been put in place,

Dennis Cross

An American Airlines 747, converted with a trapeze, a new tail assembly, and internal stiffening for carting the space shuttles around, gained fame as "The Odd Couple." Used primarily for returning the shuttle to the launch pad, it can also support training.

Dean Slaybaugh

Iraqi Airways has among the most striking of markings seen on an airliner. The stylized birds on the tail, both in color and form, are reminiscent of the old Ozark swallows, but otherwise there is no similarity in the markings.

The new series 400, with the flying wingtip, appears somewhat larger than the older series 300, as evidenced by this KLM aircraft on a test flight near Seattle, Washington.

Qantas, with one of the best aviation safety records in the business, uses the SP for long haul routes. Added to the basic markings are "Official Carrier Brisbane 1982" stickers on this aircraft, which is seen as it arrives in Honolulu, Hawaii, from Sydney, Australia.

Although not one of the early users of the 747, Air Thailand eventually came to use the aircraft for international routes out of Bangkok. Here is one of its new series 400 aircraft.

747 Braniff Place was one of the most elegant addresses available in Dallas for the many years that Braniff operated ''Big Orange'' on its Honolulu routes.

PeoplExpress used the 747 for travel between New York (Newark) and London on what amounted to a space available basis. You could go to the airport, for a very cheap price, with a no-frills ticket to London if any seats were available.

Recently Scandinavian Airline Systems (SAS) changed its markings to a more stylish fin flash under the forward fuselage for each of the member countries: from front to back, Denmark, Norway, and Sweden.

so that better and more detailed inspections can be completed. Additionally, the United Nations Security Council has called for those nations that manufacture plastic explosives to develop the technology to make the discovery of such explosives simpler.

In other areas, the commission closed the idea that somehow government agencies had more information about threats than regular citizens. The commission was also able to make specific recommendations to the State Department concerning warnings to other American international flights and treatment of survivors, which was one of the consistent areas of complaint by the survivors. Of course, as already noted, the State Department and Pan Am were not prepared for the tragedy. But, to the survivors at least, it seemed neither cared. Although in a tragedy such as this, with sensitivities and understanding stretched to the limit, the commission was at least able to suggest specific actions to minimize misunderstanding and confusion.

Rocket Attack

Unfortunately, the loss of an airliner full of passengers due to a rocket attack is not all that unusual either. In countries such as Rhodesia, Malawi, and Afghanistan, rocket attacks by various rebel groups, on aircraft such as the Viscount, Skyvan, AN-24, and IL-14, are well-known. In many cases, rockets have been suspected but not proven. Probably the most unique of such events was the deliberate destruction of a commercial airliner by the Soviet Air Force. This occurred in the late evening of 1 September 1983. Unlike most stories involving commercial airliners, this incident has strange and unusual conversations. While tapes from another disaster might record, "Twelve degrees flaps, check." tapes from this one state "Aircraft destroyed." Where tapes from another might say; "We're going in, Larry," tapes from this case state "I am breaking off."

Korean Airlines has the distinction of being the only carrier to have had one of their 747s blasted out of the sky by a Soviet air-to-air missle. HK7445, seen here, was not the aircraft destroyed in that attack, although the two airliners looked identical save for the registration number. HK7445 was, of course, destroyed in a separate accident in Seoul.

In spite of the visibility associated with the incident, and all of the drum-beating and sabre-rattling afterward, for the record at least relatively few facts are known. Korean Airlines Flight 007, a 747 outbound from San Francisco to Seoul, Korea, disappeared enroute, with all passengers and crew. The aircraft, HL-7442, departed Anchorage outbound for Seoul after an enroute stop. It disappeared with 269 souls, passengers and crew, aboard. Beyond this, little is known with the absolute certainty associated with the recovery of the CVR or the ACR. By consensus, we know that the aircraft, after having strayed into Soviet airspace, was shot down by an all-weather interceptor fighter. To this the Soviet Union agrees, although they claim that Flight 007 could not be properly identified as an airliner. According to voice tapes from both the U.S. and the Soviet Union, a Su-15 intercepted the 747, also called a "bogie." The "bogie," according to Soviet Air Force, would not respond to repeated attempts to warn or halt it. Unlighted on that dark and lonely night just off the coast of Sakalin, Soviet Air Force Major Kazmin carried out the instructions of his immediate superiors and launched an Aphid AA-9 air-to-air missile. It is believed that one or two of these missiles hit the KAL 747, probably on the left engines. What happened next can only be speculated, as the black box was never recovered. Even so, there are many anecdotal accounts of the crash, including those allegedly from Japanese fishermen who saw the aircraft strike the water. Some seem to suggest the aircraft was flying upside down, with full power to at least two engines.

Several books have been written that claim to identify some deep and mysterious reason for the incident. One of the most interesting purports to demonstrate that there was a

A Japan Airlines SR version of the 747, which was similar to this series 246B photographed at Tokyo Narita, experienced a pressure bulkhead failure and crashed near Tokyo.

massive coverup. Interestingly, the book that claims to detail this has a photograph of an aircraft on the cover. The book cover, rendered in rather fuzzy detail, clearly shows a Convair 990, so how accurate this book might be in describing a so-called coverup of a 747 may only be surmised by the reader. In any event, the books differ only in details as to exactly why the aircraft was off course, and causes of speculation have ranged from intentional misnavigation by the crew to save gas, to a variety of mistakes. Recently, an American court found Korean airlines negligent in this case. However, all accounts agree on the basics: The aircraft was off course, penetrated Soviet airspace and was subsequently shot down by the Soviet Air Force.

Tokyo

No accident involving a *single* 747 caused more loss of life than the disintegration of a Japan Airlines flight between Tokyo and Osaka. Involved was one of the Short Range aircraft, specifically designed to trade number of people for range. In other words, it could carry a lot of people, but not very far.

This aircraft had suffered a particularly hard landing, which had damaged the aft section forward of the vertical tail. It was returned for repairs, which, as Boeing later announced (by the time the rest of us guessed) might not have been completely adequate. Although technically the crash resulted from hydraulic failure, which rendered the huge aircraft uncontrollable, the real reason was due to a bulkhead failure. This failure initially caused deterioration of the rudder control, which led to deteriorated roll control. By disengaging autopilot, the crew was able to juggle a combination of engine and wing surface controls to gain some measure of real control, although with a marked tendency to fly to the right. Basically, it appeared that they were capable of reducing the oscillations that the aircraft was experiencing and could change the heading. Gradually, as the hydraulic fluid leaked from the aircraft, the remaining flying controls became ineffective. The crew had reversed heading and were enroute back to attempt a landing at Haneda. During this time, however, the hydraulics were failing as fluid leaked from the aircraft, and sometime after they apparently lowered the flaps, they were no longer able to control the aircraft. Flying about 125 miles per hour, it crashed into the mountains south of Tokyo at about 5000 feet. There were no survivors among the passengers and crew.

Because Japan Airlines was intimately involved in the inspection process, this admission had the impact of involving the Japanese in the process. Indeed, the Japanese government did find that Boeing, JAL, and the Japanese Government were probably all to some greater or lesser extent responsible for the accident. One result of this accident has been establishment of a working group in Japan that concerns itself with the problems associated with trying to control aircraft after enroute hydraulic failures. This has included not only recommendations for more and better and more frequent inspection and verification processes, but specific recommendations for the maintenance of aging aircraft.

Aging Aircraft

The 747 does not fit the category of aging aircraft in the same sense that the 737 or 727 do. By this, I mean that there are relatively few incidents of the aircraft structurally failing, and *no* instances where such a failure has involved passenger or crew fatalities. As previously discussed, the 747 began as an aircraft that had notable engine problems.

Besides the inaugural flight already discussed, there were many instances of engine failure, either due to a compressor stage rupture or a fire. After the aircraft were re-engined, these problems diminished.

Concerning engine problems, it is interesting to note that a significant number of them have been found to involve the number four engine. Although some effort was made to strengthen the pylon-to-engine structure after 1974, as a result of a specific incident involving a British aircraft, no significant design changes resulted. More common now are either cabin wiring or plumbing problems, or small pieces falling off the aircraft.

Pieces falling off aircraft are not truly an uncommon sight, either, and because the 747 is a relatively large aircraft with a *lot* of pieces, not surprisingly, pieces sometimes fall off it. Particularly common are pieces of the wings, which undergo most of the stress during normal flight operations, and the landing gear. There have been a large number of failures involving wing parts, typically a piece of one of the inboard flaps, but sometimes from an engine pylon or elsewhere on the wing. These can be inspection plates that were not properly affixed after the inspection process, or they can be movable surfaces. On 2 October 1988, a British 747 (G-BDXJ) did land in Hong Kong airport with the port gear door missing, but large pieces like this are relatively uncommon compared to the flap problems reported through the years. The 747 became part of the aging aircraft study because it is a high-use aircraft, several hulls approaching or having already passed 20 years in age.

There was a serious incident involving United Airlines Flight 811, outbound from Honolulu International Airport on 24 February 1989. Shortly after the hull was pressurized, the aircraft experienced an explosive decompression. The decompression resulted

Syria is the only country that has issued a stamp commemorating airline hijackings. Although none of their aircraft hulls have yet been destroyed, it is interesting to note that they name their aircraft after specific revolutionary dates of recent Moslem significance.

from a failure of the forward cargo door, which blew out of the aircraft and took a sizable portion of the upper passenger deck and part of the side of the aircraft as well. Nine passengers, still strapped to their seats, were swept away and killed. The aircraft returned safely to Honolulu, and no one else was hurt.

This was not the first time such a failure had been experienced on a Boeing 747. On 10 March 1978, a Pan American Airlines flight enroute from London to New York experienced similar problems. In this case, the flight crew found that they were unable to fully pressurize the aircraft. Upon returning to Chicago, they discovered that the cargo door had failed. As a result of this event, the mechanism for the cargo door latching required modifications per FAA recommendations. The particular 747 involved in the UAL incident was required to be modified prior to 30 December 1989. In the case of this particular aircraft, clearly the recommendation was inadequate.

Even so, with the incident involving the Aloha 737 (see TAB book No. 20618, *Boeing 737*), the 747, which is virtually the same age in years, came under the task force microscope. Those elements that contribute most heavily to reducing the life cycle of the aircraft, namely landing and takeoff cycles and pollution, are less a factor in an aircraft like a 747 than in an aircraft like a 737. This is because the 747 typically flies considerably farther, therefore taking off and landing many fewer times, and because it spends longer at higher altitude, those carbon and sulfur compounds that so greatly contribute to the corrosion and fatigue of a metal airframe are much less of a factor. But the basic problem—how to make the airframe last for a long time—remains the same.

One of the recent impacts of this problem that we are seeing is that established carriers with older aircraft are selling them and buying newer aircraft. Many of these older aircraft are going to all-cargo carriers or nonscheduled passenger carriers, many of whom are now flying the older 707s and DC-8s. It does not take long, reading through a yearly accident summary, to see that these jets are more frequently involved in accidents than established passenger carriers. Part of the reason is probably due to the fact that the aircraft are often landing at fields where the crew never previously landed, or fields that have unusual landing considerations, but it would be a misunderstanding not to recognize that in at least some cases, maintenance is a contributing cause.

Based on these problems, it will not be particularly surprising to see nonpassenger-carrying 747s involved in future accidents, such as the Flying Tigers 747 that crashed on approach into Singapore on 19 February 1989.

The Future

With new 747s just rolling off the assembly lines, and with earlier 747s still being upgraded, there is no doubt that we will continue to see them in the news for years still to come.

Additionally, with the cost of a new 747 at $125 million or more, and the cost of completely overhauling an aircraft being about a tenth as much, we can expect to see all series of 747s around for some time to come. A good example of this was an Air France aircraft, which was not overhauled until 1989, after a hard landing in which it incurred substantial damage in New Delhi. Ordinarily, there is a good chance that the aircraft would have been scrapped or sold for parts. But the scarcity of jumbo jets, combined with the long wait for a new one, make it profitable to repair damaged aircraft. One of the main delays in this case was caused by the lack of available Boeing engineers, all of whom were tied up with the series 400 development and production.

Other recent changes in the philosophy of major carriers show that when the aircraft approaches about 20 flying years, it will become more expensive to maintain than a new aircraft will be to operate. For this reason, you will see more and more examples of carriers such as Japan Airlines selling their high-time airframes to cargo and nonscheduled carriers. Considering the youth of the aircraft and the fact that new versions are still on the drawing boards, we can expect to see the 747 in the news for years to come.

6

In Scale

B ECAUSE the 747 has been around and popular for quite a while, there is a rather large number of kits and decals from which to choose if you wish to model it. Identified in TABLE 6-1, by kit number, scale, and markings, are those known to me. In many cases, the same model is offered by a particular vendor in a variety of markings, and in some few cases, the same model is offered in the same or different markings by more than one vendor. The comparative rarity of each kit is indicated by a numerical rating, wherein 4 is readily available, 3 somewhat available, 2 hardly available, and 1 is scarce.

Because of the large variety of kits available, the comments in the next section will be limited to those kits which are, or have been, readily available, primarily in 1/200 and 1/144 scales, although several interesting models have been available in other scales.

1/200 Scale

Although marketed under a variety of different brand names and in a variety of markings, without a doubt, the best 1/200 scale 747 on the market is by Hasegawa. This model has been distributed in several different versions, including Pratt and Whitney engines, Rolls Royce engines, and as series 100, 200, and 300 aircraft. In addition, it has been available from Minicraft and Hobbycraft with the General Electric engines. The specific model discussed here is the original series 100, but all of the other versions are quite similar.

Comprising 56 parts, molded in both solid and clear plastic, the kit fits well and is easily assembled. The only clear part for the fuselage is the front windscreen. In some but not all kits, there is included a two-piece clear plastic stand. In reality, the "clear" is not clear at all, but as with most Hasegawa airliners, smoked. The rest of the parts are in regular injection-molded medium-hard styrene, which will vary in color, depending on the

Table 6-1. Boeing 747 model kits by manufacturer, scale, and markings.
Rarity is rated from 1 (very rare) to 4 (currently commonly available).

Maker	Kit Number	Series	Scale	Markings	Rarity
Academy	1640	100	1/288	NASA w/shuttle	3
Academy	1640	100	1/288	NASA w/o shuttle	3
Academy	1641	100	1/288	PAA	3
Advent	3402	200	1/144	TWA (golden globes)	2
Airfix	4318	200	1/144	Qantas (Australian issue)	2
Airfix	SK811	100	1/144	BOAC	3
Airfix	08174	100	1/144	Lufthansa	3
Airfix	08174	100	1/144	British Airways/Alitalia	3
Airfix	909174	100	1/144	British Airways	4
Airfix	908170	100	1/144	British Airways	4
Airfix	908173	100	1/144	Braniff "Big Orange"	3
Airfix	08170-2	100	1/144	BOAC	2
Airfix	08170-2	100	1/144	British Airways	2
Airfix	08171-5	100	1/144	Lufthansa	2
Airfix	08172-8	100	1/144	Air France	2
Airfix	08173/1	100	1/144	Braniff "Big Orange"	2
Airfix	08174-4	200	1/144	Qantas	2
Airfix	08173-1	100	1/144	Braniff "Big Orange"	3
Airfix	unk	200	1/144	E4B Flying Whitehouse	3
Anmark	7553	100	1/100	TWA	1
Anmark	7567	100	1/100	UAL	2
Araii	89C	100	1/288	PAA/JAL	2
Aurora	358	100	1/156	Braniff	2
Aurora	360	100	1/156	Delta	2
Aurora	360	100	1/156	KLM	2
Aurora	360KL	100	1/156	KLM (Netherlands issue)	2
Aurora	361	100	1/156	Braniff	2
Aurora	361	100	1/156	PAA	2
Aurora	361	100	1/156	Continental	1
Aurora	361	100	1/156	CP Air	1
Aurora	361-1	100	1/156	British Airways	2
Aurora	362	100	1/156	United Airlines	2
Aurora	363	100	1/156	TWA	2
Aurora	379	100	1/156	Continental	2
Aurora	383	100	1/156	CP Air	1
Bienengräber	set	100	1/380	Lufthansa	2
Challenge	7266	200	1/72	n/a, vacuum formed kit	1
Crown	253	100	1/380	JAL	2
Doyusha	100-B4	100	1/100	UAL/ANA	4
Doyusha	unk	100	1/100	Lufthansa	4
Doyusha	B001	100	1/100	Japan Airlines	4
Entex	8453	100	1/100	TWA	1

Maker	Kit Number	Series	Scale	Markings	Rarity
Entex	8453	100	1/100	UAL	1
Entex	8496J	100	1/540	TWA	2
Entex	8496J	100	1/540	PAA	2
Entex	8560	100	1/144	Flying Tigers/UAL	2
Fuji	071	100	1/540	ANA	1
Fuiji	072	100	1/540	JAL	1
Fuyimi	F1	100	1/400	ANA	2
General Mills	n/a	100	1/273	PAA	1
Ikko	251	100	1/240	NWO w/motor	3
Ikko	261	100	1/240	NWO w/o motor	3
KSN/Midori	13	100	1/288	Pan American	3
KSN/Midori	14	100	1/288	Japan Airlines	3
Hasegawa	D001	100	1/200	Japan Airlines	4
Hasegawa	D002	100	1/200	Pan American	4
Hasegawa	D003	200	1/200	Air France	4
Hasegawa	D004	200	1/200	Lufthansa	4
Hasegawa	D005	200	1/200	Singapore	4
Hasegawa	D006	200	1/200	South African Airways	4
Hasegawa	D007	200	1/200	All Nippon Airways	4
Hasegawa	D008	300	1/200	Singapore (Bip Top)	4
Hasegawa	D009	200	1/200	Qantas	4
Hasegawa	D010	200	1/200	United Air Lines	4
Hasegawa	D011	300	1/200	KLM	4
Hasegawa	D012	200	1/200	Pan American	4
Hasegawa	1131	100	1/200	Air Canada	4
Heller	L.037	100	1/450	Air France	2
Heller	L.037	100	1/450	KLM	2
Heller	037	100	1/450	Air France	4
Heller	80037	100	1/450	KLM	4
Heller	L.856	100	1/125	Air France	2
Heller	L.856	100	1/125	KLM (Dutch issue)	1
Heller	L.856	100	1/125	Swissair	2
Heller	L.856	100	1/125	Air France/Swissair	1
Heller	L.856	100	1/125	Air France/Qantas	1
Heller	459	100	1/125	Air France/SAS	3
Heller	463	100	1/125	KLM (Dutch issue)	1
Heller	468	100	1/125	Swissair	4
Heller	470	100	1/125	Air France	2
Heller	856	100	1/125	Air France/Swissair	1
Heller	80459	100	1/125	Air France	4
Hobbycraft	1131	100	1/200	Air Canada	4
Idea	AP037	200	1/200	Northwest Orient	4
IKKO	251	100	1/240	Northwest Orient	1
IKKO	261	100	1/240	Northwest Orient	1
Kawai	KJP05	100	1/1040	JAL	1

Maker	Kit Number	Series	Scale	Markings	Rarity
Kawai	KJP06	100	1/1040	PAA	1
KOGA	KO-35	100	1/150	JAL	2
KOGA	KO-81	100	1/150	JAL/Lufthansa	2
KSN/Midori	13	100	1/288	PAA/TAP	1
KSN/Midori	14	100	1/288	JAL	1
KSN/Midori	747	100	1/288	PAA	1
KSN/Midori	200	100	1/288	JAL	1
Landex	unk	200	1/300	Korean Air Lines	2
Landex	unk	200	1/300	JAL	2
Landex	unk	200	1/300	Singapore Airlines	2
Lodela	RO-8037	100	1/450	Air France/KLM	4
Minicraft	1170	100	1/200	Pan American	3
Monogram	5412	100	1/156	PAA	3
MPC	1-4751	100	1/144	PAA	3
MPC	1-4752	100	1/144	UAL	3
MPC	1-4753	100	1/144	TWA	3
MPC	2-3300	100	1/144	AA	3
Nitto	159	100	1/144	JAL	2
Nitto	200	100	1/144	PAA	2
Nitto	301	100	1/540	Pan American	2
Nitto	311	100	1/200	JAL	2
Nitto	340	100	1/100	JAL/Lufthansa	1
Nitto	700	200	1/100	ANA	1
Nitto	723	100	1/390	JAL	2
Nitto	732	100	1/144	ANA	2
Nitto	754	100	1/200	ANA	2
Otaki	OT-2-32	200	1/350	PAA	2
Otaki	OT-2-33	200	1/350	JAL	2
Otaki	OT-2-34	200	1/350	Alitalia	2
Otaki	OT-2-35	200	1/350	Lufthansa	2
Otaki	OT-2-36	200	1/350	KLM	2
Otaki	OT-2-37	200	1/350	Singapore	2
Revell (Ger)	0171	100	1/144	KLM	1
Revell (Ger)	0175	100	1/144	Lufthansa (cutaway)	1
Revell (Ger)	0176	100	1/144	Lufthansa	1
Revell (US)	3402	100	1/144	TWA (golden globes)	2
Revell (Eur)	3402	100	1/144	TWA/Swissair	2
Revell (Ger)	4205	100	1/144	SAS	2
Revell (Ger)	4208	100	1/144	Swissair	4
Revell (Ger)	4223	100	1/144	KLM	4
Revell (Ger)	4228	100	1/144	Lufthansa	4
Revell (Ger)	4248	100	1/288	NASA w/shuttle	4
Revell (Ger)	4507	100	1/144	Sabena/Lufthansa	4
Revell (Spn)	4513	100	1/144	Iberia (cutaway)	1
Revell (Mxc)	4513	100	1/144	Aerolineas Argentinas	2

Maker	Kit Number	Series	Scale	Markings	Rarity
Revell (US)	H-136	100	1/144	TWA (golden globes)	2
Revell (Mxc)	H-136	100	1/144	TWA (golden globes)	2
Revell (Mxc)	H-138	100	1/144	Flying Tigers	1
Revell (Ger)	H-171	100	1/144	SAS	2
Revell (Ger)	H-171	100	1/144	KLM	2
Revell (Ger)	H-175	100	1/144	Lufthansa (cutaway)	2
Revell (UK)	H-175	100	1/144	Lufthansa (cutaway)	2
Revell (Jap)	H-175	100	1/144	Lufthansa	2
Revell (Mxc)	H-175	100	1/144	Lufthansa	3
Revell (Ntl)	H-176	100	1/144	Lufthansa/Sabena	1
Revell (Ger)	H-176	100	1/144	Lufthansa	2
Revell (Sws)	H-176	100	1/144	Lufthansa/Swissair	1
Revell (Jap)	H-176	100	1/144	Lufthansa	3
Revell (Jap)	H-176	100	1/144	ANA	1
Revell (Mxc)	H-176	100	1/144	Aerolineas Argentinas	1
Revell (UK)	H-177	100	1/144	British/SAS (cutaway)	2
Revell (US)	UAL	100	1/144	UAL (cutaway)	2
Revell (Mxc)	RH-4223	100	1/144	KLM	4
Revell (Mxc)	RH-4513	100	1/144	Aerolineas Argentinas	4
Revell (US)	unk	100	1/144	NASA w/Atlantis	3
Revell (US)	unk	100	1/144	E4B	3
Starfix	201	100	1/293	El Al	2
Toho	34	100	1/150	Boeing	1
Toho	35	100	1/150	Japan Airlines	1
Toho	81	100	1/288	Japan Airlines	2
USAirfix	6101	100	1/144	Braniff	2

Conversions

Maker	Kit Number	Series	Scale	Markings	Rarity
AA/ATP	747SUD	300	1/144	Resin upper deck (Revell kit)	4
Airtec	n/a	SP	1/144	expanded foam (Revell kit)	1
A. Hess	n/a	SP	1/144	filled resin (Revell kit)	1
Sasquatch	SQ-22	SP	1/200	injection (Hasegawa kit)	4

particular kit. In general, the fuselage and tail assembly are white plastic, while the wings and engines are light gray. Although other colors are possible, since they are all fairly light, they take an airliner finish easily.

This kit, like others in this "Loveliner" 1/200 series, provides a number of engineering innovations that are intended to simplify assembly. One of them is that the cockpit windscreen is to be added to the model after assembly is completed. However, the fit is a bit tight, and if you add it after painting, you might want to either mask or scrape the paint away from the inner part of the assembly, as otherwise the windscreen will probably not fit.

The fuselage is made of two parts, split down the center, and assembly is straightforward. Little putty is required, which is good, because with the external antennas molded in place, it is difficult to sand the model if any putty is used. One of the interesting innovations presented by Hasegawa for this model is a fuselage former, which doubles as a nose weight holder. There is no interior detail, although in this scale and through the smoked plastic, none would be visible anyway.

Assembly of the wings and engines is also straightforward, with the wings being represented in three parts, one lower and two upper halves; the engines are in two separate parts, with front nacelles pieces including the fans. The engine fan assembly has a ridge around the circumference due to the molding process. The appearance of the model will be improved if this is sanded and polished off before painting. In another of the engineering innovations, Hasegawa has presented the landing gear doors as part of the gear assembly itself. Although this leaves the doors way out of scale, on a model of this size the result is not unsatisfactory, and the ease of assembly and painting is great.

Through the life of this model, it has been issued with an extended upper deck and other engines besides the original Pratt and Whitney versions, but all of the basic assembly stays the same. The landing gear is overscale but quite sturdy, and will easily support the model. One of the shortcomings of molding the landing gear in this manner is that it almost forces the builder to model the plane with the gear down, unless new doors are fashioned.

In overall outline and presentation, the model looks very much like a 747, and scales out very well. One of the most prominent features, the front windscreen, is somewhat too deep in the front, causing the overall outline to appear more droop-nosed than it should.

Converted to an SP before the availability of the Sasquatch conversion kit, which makes the entire job a lot easier, this photo shows the very fine detail on the Hasegawa 1/200 scale kit.

You might wish to correct this by puttying and painting the correct outline, or by completely filling in all of the windows and using decals. If you take this latter route, be sure to glue a strip of plastic in behind the cabin windows before you fill them with putty, or you can be sure that the putty will come out of at least some of the windows during the course of finishing the model.

Decals for all of the Japanese versions are excellent; they are thin, adhere well, and contain all of the necessary fuselage door and window outlines. Other versions are not as good; although the Minicraft version has decals made by Scalemaster, they are not as complete as the Japanese versions in terms of exit markings and choice of registrations.

1/144 Scale

Several different 1/144 scale models have been marketed, and I will only discuss the three most common ones here.

Nitto. Considering the excellence of their 1/100 scale model, Nitto's 1/144 scale model is terrible. The model is also probably the same one marketed by both Toho and Entex variously at 1/150 and 1/144 scales. It actually scales at closer to 1/150, and the overall attention to detail and the outline are simply abysmal. This model represents the series 100 with the three-window upper deck and General Electric engines. It comprises 87 parts, molded in clear and white plastic, with some versions of the kit having black plastic wheels. Some versions also come with a separate clear plastic two-piece stand for supporting the model while in "flight," either with the gear up or down.

Although it might seem that the model has a lot of parts, a full 27 of them are clear parts, including four landing lights, one front windscreen, and a variety of cabin window

David H Minton

Possibly the worst model of the 747 ever made, the 1/144 Nitto kit only vaguely resembles the actual 747, particularly around the nose and engine areas. The kit decals, although thick, can be used.

parts. Of the remaining parts, 28 of them are wheels and gear, eight are gear doors, and 16 are engine parts, four for each of four engines. The fit of the parts is not very good, with filling and sanding needed at almost every joint, except where the landing gear glues to the gear well.

In overall outline, the fuselage is truly astounding in its inaccuracy. Although the attempt is to model the early three-window upper version, there is no satellite bulge provided, and the outline of the cockpit is so inaccurate as to make the model more closely resemble an ATL 98 than any 747! Although there is a wide variety of decals and markings available for this model, including from other kits, it is not a 747 to seek out.

Airfix. For some reason, Airfix also made a pretty bad model of the 747, and has continued to produce it through the years. Presumably it is a good seller. In addition to the Airfix label, the kit has been made available through USAirfix and MPC. The model represents the series 100 with the three-window upper deck. Certainly it is considerably better than the Nitto kit, Airfix having achieved at least an approximation of the correct fuselage outline. There is a total of 126 parts, usually molded in clear and white plastic, although some kits were marketed in light gray. Some versions of the kit, particularly those marketed in the UK, came with a two-piece black plastic Airfix model stand. Although there are 35 clear parts, including all of the cabin windows and the front windscreen, all of them are thick and unclear in appearance. The front windscreen, which is the only clear part that must be used, is particularly thick and incorrectly rendered, being set much too deeply toward the rear of the aircraft.

From an engineering point of view, as a model, this kit actually has only one interesting innovation, which is present on all Airfix airliner models. This innovation is called a punch tool, and it is used to punch out the cheat line decal after it has been applied to the model. If, however, you later craft your windows with Krystal Kleer or some similar white

Seen with Micro Scale decals, this Airfix model shows the problems associated with the engine nacelles and the fuselage outline of this 1/144 scale kit. With effort, it can be made acceptable.

glue, you will probably find parts of the decal floating in your clear windows. One way around this is to paint the decal residue into the window outline using Pactra Aero Gloss thinner or some similar solvent.

The most obvious problem with this model is in the engine nacelle area. Although each assembly is made up of four parts in a more-or-less conventional form, they look terrible. Perhaps the engines were modeled with the thrust reversers deployed, or perhaps the Airfix engineers attempted something unusual with the engines. They are molded with left and right halves, with front nacelles and afterbodies, and are made to resemble the early Pratt and Whitney fans. Each left and right half includes the engine pylons, which are the same for all four engines. They are also grossly incorrect for all four engines and should be modified. The engine front part, which includes an integrally molded fan, also has a spurious groove completely around the circumference of the engine. This must be filled and sanded smooth, making a uniform metal finish on the nacelle even more difficult than might be expected. In summary, the engines and pylons are incorrect and will require significant filling, reshaping, and sanding of each to achieve anything that looks even approximately correct.

Many of the remaining parts are simply detail pieces, and most do very little to add to the appearance of the model because the original detail on the model is so vague. For example, 11 separate parts are provided for some of the cabin and cargo doors. Because nowhere on the model is the fit particularly good, you can expect to spend a significant amount of time filling, filing, and sanding all of the joints, including the cargo doors, which are especially accurate. The same is true for the wing-to-fuselage joints, the tail-to-fuselage joints, the engine pylons, the engines, and for all of the cabin doors. There is also an interior bulkhead fitted, presumably to prevent fuselage deformation and to contribute to the fit. On the contrary, it is slightly oversized, and will have to be filed down to be used without itself warping the fuselage! The flap tracks are provided as individual parts for each wing, and although in the most general sense they resemble the real thing, the fit is so bad that you will need to spend a lot of time worrying with them before gluing them to the wing.

Similarly, the wing-to-fuselage joint, which is supported by a plastic tab of adequate size for a model about half the size of this one, will need work. The wings will fit the fuselage at a variety of angles and positions, with a multitude of possibilities for wing misalignment. As with all of these 747 models, if you are going to position the model with the gear down and sitting on the ground, you will want to be careful to achieve proper alignment of all of the relevant parts so that the wheels will all touch the surface. Thanks to the poor fit of the Airfix model, and the ill-fitted slots, this job is almost impossible, so plan extra time to get it right.

This kit is most often presented in soft white plastic, although it has also been seen in other colors. Because the plastic is relatively soft, it does not take a very good metal finish and you might want to consider primer. However, because it is light in color, at least it is possible to get a fairly good airliner finish on it.

The decals provided with most versions of the Airfix kit are generally usable, although, as discussed later in this section, there is a variety of aftermarket decals available.

Revell. Without doubt, the Revell kit is the best 1/144 scale 747 on the market. In addition to the various versions marketed by Revell Germany, Revell Brazil, Revell Mexico, Revell Japan, Revell Europe, and Revell USA, this kit has also been marketed by

Advent. It has been produced as a variety of versions in the series 100 and 200, with both the three-upper-cabin-window and the ten upper-cabin-window-arrangements. It comprises 72 total parts, including one clear front windscreen. The remaining parts are in relatively hard white plastic. As a result, the model takes any metal or painted airliner finish easily. There is also a white plastic four-piece stand. If the stand is not used, there is an optional support for the rear of the fuselage to hold the model properly on its gear. As usual, if the model is to be displayed on its gear, take care to align everything so the airplane sits properly on the wheels.

Twenty of the parts are for the engine nacelles, including the pylons; another 27 parts are associated with the landing gear, including 18 wheels. The overall fit of the parts is adequate, with a bit of filler and sanding needed on most of the main joints, particularly the upper fuselage joint near the upper cabin. The windows are drilled out, and although there are no clear parts for the windows, some of the decal films have clear portions for the windows on the cheat lines. You will probably not want to use any of these, instead punching out the decal and using Krystal Kleer or the like, because the clear decals are not very clear, nor are they very strong.

The engines are made up of the left and right halves, with the fan in front, and left and right nacelle and pylon halves. The center portion of the nacelle is the same as the outer portion of the engine, which although not correct, can be made to look acceptable with care. The landing gear is rudimentary, but strong enough for the model; it may be positioned in either an up or down configuration.

Without doubt, the Revell kit is the best 1/144 scale kit available in terms of scale and detail. It also comes with a wide variety of very usable decals. This model was completed with Revell of Germany kit decals. The cheat lines were painted and the windows filled in with Krystal Kleer.

The overall shape and appearance of the model is quite acceptable and the model scales out very close to 1/144 scale in all dimensions. The decals provided with most versions of the model are complete and thin enough to be easily usable, although some of those from the South American countries have a slightly yellowish film, which looks bad on a white crown. There is a great variety of decals available from other sources, as discussed below.

1/156 Scale

The Aurora kit can be used to build a model in this scale, if you are interested in modeling one of the early "box scale" airliners. This model is called "box scale" because it dates from the days when models were scaled to fit the size of the production box and not to any set scale associated with model collecting. This is probably the first model of the 747 that was widely available, and although the molds were later cleaned up and the model reissued by Monogram, basically no improvement took place throughout the mold's life. The only changes were in the decals and the box art.

It is made up of 63 total parts, although some kits also came with a two-piece clear plastic stand. Also, there is a clear part for the front windscreen. The solid plastic, which makes up 62 parts, is usually light colored (stark white through light cream to gray) and is pretty hard, so it will easily take a metal finish. The cabin windows are hollowed out, but no clear parts are provided. The fit of the parts is typical of an early model, and there is usually at least some flash present on most of the pieces. In addition, the seams may be somewhat uneven.

The fuselage is two major parts, left and right half, including the vertical tail. The engines are made up of four parts, left and right halves, including the pylons. The pylons are the same for both the inboard and outboard engines, which is incorrect, and you will want to correct this problem with scrap plastic. The engines themselves are only generally like the GE engines on the early production aircraft, and both the nacelles and the afterbodies are pretty rough. The fit of the wing-fuselage joint is worse than most of the rest of the model. The model will want a lot of weight in the nose if you are going to sit it on its rather rudimentary gear. With all 747 kits, which have five landing gear, alignment is important to get the model to sit correctly on the gear, but with the Aurora offering, this is especially critical.

Decals are a problem, insofar as the only 1/156 scale decals available are from the original kits. Although the original decals were in some cases fairly good, in many other cases they were pretty bad, and by now, typically useless. In any event, the original decals for most models provided only the most basic of the markings, including the logo and a cheat line. Actually, however, the model scales out with the fuselage closer to 1/156 and the wing and tail assembly larger, about 1/150. This makes the model pretty close to 1/144 overall, and you could probably get by using 1/144 scale decals for many marking choices, save for the door and exit markings.

1/125 Scale

The basic Heller kit, which is also used as the basis for several other 1/125 scale models, can be used to make a satisfactory model in this relatively uncommon scale. The model itself is made up of 139 parts, including 30 clear parts and 109 solid parts. Those models made in France are usually in a medium-soft light gray plastic, which makes it relatively easy to put the aircraft livery on, but relatively difficult for a good metal finish. A primer might help to get a uniform metal finish on this type of plastic. Although the fit is acceptable throughout the model, the thick and slightly misaligned trailing edges and oversized parts are a persistent problem. Virtually every seam, except for the leading edges of the flying surfaces, will probably need at least a little putty and sanding, unless you received an unusually good press job. With time and patience, however, the overall outline and appearance of the finished product is quite acceptable, particularly given the amount of detail included on the model. Control surface details are engraved lines, and only the most prominent surfaces of the fuselage are provided as raised lines.

Many of the parts make up the details of the main and wing landing gear assemblies. There are a total of four, each of which has at least a main gear strut and four wheels, as well as several ancillary tubes and reinforcement struts or side stays. Of all the models available, this one probably has the most detailed landing gear assemblies. Additionally, for the main gear there is an additional square part at the top, which makes the entire assembly stronger.

Other engineering innovations do not necessarily make the job easier. Probably most annoying is the fact that the fuselage itself is made up of four parts, split vertically down the center in the conventional fashion, but split horizontally across the vertical axis at about the center trailing forward flap location. Although this technique somewhat reduces the possibility of fuselage warpage, it creates more joints that need to be filled and increases the possibility of misalignment. It is notched at the cabin window location, and, in general, is not an easy assembly to achieve. I recommend assembling the entire fuselage at once, rather than trying to do it as two major subassemblies. There are separate wheel well assemblies for both the main and nose gear, so be sure to get them before you glue the fuselage parts together. It will take a considerable amount of weight in the nose to keep the model on its gear, although a clear strut is provided to glue to the lower fuselage for stabilization if you prefer that method.

The engines are made up of five parts each, which include the engine assembly itself (left and right halves), the engine nacelle (same), and the fan. The engine sits between the nacelles, and the sidewall of the engine assembly is, in fact, the corresponding part for the engine nacelle. This is neither accurate nor particularly pleasing on the finished model, but with careful fitting and painting can be made to look acceptable.

The front windscreen is separate, but unlike many of the Heller airliners, it does not include the upper part of the fuselage. Although the fit is not exceptionally good, it is not as difficult as some of their other airliners. Decals are a problem, unless you want to use one of the usually French schemes which come with the model. There are very few 1/125 decals, so for something different, your best bet would be to adapt and use decals from another kit or source.

1/100 Scale

The Nitto kit, which was available in United Airlines (current colors) markings, is a series 100 version with the three-window upper deck and General Electric engines. It has also been marketed by Otaki and Doyusha in various other markings. It is molded in white and black medium-hard plastic. There is a total of 402 parts, including 39 clear parts. The front windscreen comprises three separate parts, with side pieces for each pair of side windows and one part for the main front center piece. There is a four-piece black plastic stand, which is fitted with two upper portions to allow for adequate support for the model.

All of the windows are drilled out and there are clear parts for all of them, including the upper deck, which has a separate piece for each window. There is a rudimentary upper cabin area, including a flight deck with an instrument panel decal and a rear lounge area. Each of the main landing gear assemblies, including the wheels, is made up of 24 or more separate parts, and the model comes with four sets of chocks to display in the gear-down position. The instruction sheet contains several detailed drawings and photos of the real parts with each of the assembly sections. Engines, which represent the early Pratt and Whitney JT9D turbofans, are made up of 12 parts each.

The fit of the parts throughout the model is good, with little filing and sanding needed, except for the wing root joints. The overall model has an excellent appearance when finally finished. The decals provided with the model are more than adequate, being thin and generally well registered. If you are considering a different livery for the model, because of the size, decals might be a bit of a problem. But given the size, you might give serious consideration to painting the livery directly onto the model. All in all, this is a very pleasing model, although not very small.

Conversions

Two conversion kits have been available for the 747. Both of these will allow you to convert the model to an SP (Special Performance) version. Both were made primarily to work with the Revell kit, insofar as the parts are compatible.

The Micro West version was made of expanded foam, with three parts: an entire fuselage, including the vertical tail, and two horizontal tail parts. These fit nicely with the Revell wings and landing gear. Because the entire fuselage is one piece, it is easiest to hollow out a section in the nose for the nose gear, and at the same time rout it out so that the nose can be weighted if so desired. It is easiest to put small lead weights such as BBs up in the hole, and then cover them with epoxy or alpha cycronacalate glue. Because the fuselage is solid, it would be fairly difficult to make the model with the windows drilled out. Therefore, the easiest way to complete it is with a window decal, available from third party vendors, discussed below. The model comes with Pan Am SP decals, and includes a front windscreen.

The Alan Hess conversion is made of hand-poured filled resin. As such, it has much better surface detail and is presented in a manner similar to injection-molded kits. That is, the fuselage (including the vertical tail) is made of two parts, which must be glued together. The thickness of the resin is fairly heavy, a lot heavier than injection-molded plastic, but as a result, there is very little warpage in the model. The remaining parts consist of the two horizontal tail parts, which fit easily into the fuselage. Again, this kit is made especially to go with the Revell model, and as a result it fits very nicely with the Revell wings, engines, and gear. As with the Micro West kit, the windows are not drilled out, and doing so would prove to be extremely difficult. No decals come with the model, so these will have to be obtained from other sources. Side window decals are readily available from the sources already mentioned, but the front windscreen will have to come from some other source, or hand-painted.

Decals

Besides the decals that come in the various kits, some of which are very good, a wide variety of separate decals is available from decal vendors such as Runway 30, Jet Set Systems (including related vendors), Micro-Scale (now Super Decal), and ATP, Inc. These decals are all good and offer an opportunity to make different versions.

Runway 30 offered 1/144 scale sheets for El Al (4x-AXA), an Iraqi aircraft (YI-AGN), and a South African Airlines aircraft (ZS-SAN). These decals typically do not have the complete cheat line, and although an orange stripe is provided with the South African sheet, it is much too fluorescent to be of any use.

Jet Set offered 1/144 scale sheets for Braniff International (N9666), Trans Mediterranean of Lebanon (OD-AGC), and UTA (F-BTDG). In addition, they offer a variety of the new Air France sheets, which can be made to fit several of the various scaled 747 models.

Calcomanias Barabazon did a nice sheet for the current Avianca markings for HK-1716 and HK-2300.

ATP, Inc. offers 1/144 scale sheets for Pan Am, including N747PA and N657PA, both 121 series, and N532PA and N540PA, both of which are SP21 aircraft. The clipper names for all of the aircraft are included on the decal sheet. In addition, a very nice Transamerica sheet, for N743TV, complete with all cheat lines is provided. ATP, Inc. also has both cabin windows and front windscreens for 747 aircraft available in 1/144 scale.

Micro Scale had available four sheets in 1/144 scale. These sheets included one for NWO (N601US), JAL (JA8102) and Air Canada (CF-TOA), all 100 series; one for UAL (N4718U), PAA (N747PA), and Condor (D-ABYF), both 100 and 200 series; one for TWA (N5311), Singapore Airlines (9V-SIB), and Qantas (VH-EBA), both 100 and 200 series; and one for Air India (VT-EBE) in the original delivery markings. None of these

This A. Hess conversion kit was made using Revell kit parts for the wings, horizontal tail, engines and landing gear. Decals are adapted from the Runway 30 set for the series 200.

sheets came with cheat lines except for the Air India aircraft, which included the Hindu style window outlines.

Additionally, decals for cabin doors are available in both 1/144 and 1/200 scale from these vendors. With new versions of the 747 going into production, new decals and markings are sure to follow.

Among the easiest of conversions, for an "out-of-the-box" kit, is applying different decals on the model. There is a wide variety of decals available for the big Boeing jet. The decals applied to this Revell model came from Jet Set Systems.

Appendix
Boeing 747
Fleet Listings

Boeing 747 Fleet Listing

s/n	reg	carrier	series	ff	dd	remarks
19637	N731PA	Pan American	121	5/10/68	7/11/70	*Clipper Bostonian*
	N731PA	Eastern Airlines			1/3/71	leased
	N731PA	Pan American			4/29/71	*Clipper Bostonian*
	9Q-ARW	Zaire Aero Services			4/20/80	
	N731PA	Pan American			1980	*Clipper Bostonian*
19638	N732PA	Pan American	121	7/10/69	7/13/70	*Clipper Storm King*
19639	N747PA	Pan American	121	4/11/69	10/3/70	*Clipper America*
	N747QC	Air Zaire			11/21/73	leased, *Mont Hoyo*
	N747PA	Pan American			3/31/75	*Clipper America*
19640	N733PA	Pan American	121	10/24/69	12/13/69	*Clipper Constitution*
	N733PA	G.E.Credit Corp			6/81	
	N733PA	Pan American			6/81	leased, *Clipper Constitution*
19641	N734PA	Pan American	121	10/31/69	12/19/69	*Clipper Flying Cloud*
19642	N735PA	Pan American	121	12/22/69	1/9/70	*Clipper Young America*
	N735PA	Eastern Airlines			1/29/70	leased
	N735PA	Pan American			4/30/72	*Clipper Young America*
	N735PA	G.E. Credit Corp			6/81	
	N735PA	Pan American			6/81	leased
						Clipper Young America
19643	N736PA	Pan American	121	12/24/69	1/20/70	w/o 5/27/77 Tenerife
						Clipper Victor
19644	N737PA	Pan American	121	1/9/70	1/21/70	*Clipper Red Jacket*
	N737PA	Eastern Airlines			2/1/70	leased
	N737PA	Pan American			5/5/72	*Clipper Red Jacket*
	N737PA	G.E. Credit Corp			6/81	

s/n	reg	carrier	series	ff	dd	remarks
	N737PA	Pan American			6/81	leased, *Clipper Red Jacket*
19645	N738PA	Pan American	121	1/19/70	2/5/70	*Clipper Defender*
	N738PA	G.E. Credit Corp			6/81	
	N738PA	Pan American			6/81	leased
						w/o 10/18/83 Karachi
						Clipper Defender
19646	N739PA	Pan American	121	1/25/70	2/15/70	*Clipper Morning Light*
19647	N740PA	Pan American	121	1/31/70	2/24/70	*Clipper Revival*
	N740PA	American Airlines			2/25/70	leased
	N740PA	Pan American			5/14/71	*Clipper Revival*
	N740PA	G.E. Credit Corp			6/81	
	N740PA	Pan American			6/81	leased, *Clipper Revival*
19648	N741PA	Pan American	121	2/13/70	2/28/70	*Clipper Kit Carson*
	N741PA	G.E. Credit Corp			6/81	
	N741PA	Pan American			6/81	leased, *Clipper Kit Carson*
19649	N742PA	Pan American	121	23/18/70	3/2/70	*Clipper Rainbow*
	N742PA	G.E. Credit Corp			6/81	
	N742PA	Pan American			6/81	leased, *Clipper Rainbow*
19650	N743PA	Pan American	121	3/15/70	3/28/70	*Clipper Derby*
	N743PA	American Airlines			2/29/70	
	N743PA	Pan American			10/1/70	*Clipper Derby*
19651	N744PA	Pan American	121	3/12/70	3/21/70	*Clipper Star of the Union*
	N744PA	G.E. Credit Corp			6/81	
	N744PA	Pan American			6/81	leased
						Clipper Star of the Union
19652	N748PA	Pan American	121	3/21/70	3/31/70	*Clipper Hornet*
19653	N749PA	Pan American	121	3/29/70	4/10/70	*Clipper Intrepid*
19654	M750PA	Pan American	121	4/12/70	4/26/70	*Clipper Rambler*
19655	N751PA	Pan American	121	4/10/70	4/24/70	*Clipper Midnight Sun*
	N751PA	Evergreen International			1989	
	N751PA	Orion Air			1989	leased
19656	N752PA	Pan American	121	4/22/70	5/2/70	w/o 9/6/70 Cairo
						Clipper Fortune
19657	N753PA	Pan American	121	4/15/70	4/29/70	*Clipper West Wind*
	N753PA	Evergreen International			1989	
19658	N754PA	Pan American	121	5/2/70	5/26/70	*Clipper Ocean Rover*
19659	N755PA	Pan American	121	5/8/70	5/31/70	*Clipper Soverign of theSkies*
19660	N770PA	Pan American	121	5/7/70	5/31/70	*Clipper Great Republic*
19961	N771PA	Pan american	121	9/15/70	10/4/70	*Clipper Donald McKay*
	N771PA	Pan American	121F/SC		3/30/75	converted
	N819FT	Flying Tigers			2/83	
19667	N93101	Trans World Airlines	131	7/13/69	8/18/70	
	5-280	Imp Iranian AF (IIAF)			3/14/75	
	5-8101	IIAF	131F		7/7/75	converted
	5-8101	Iranian Air Force			2/78	
	EP-NHJ	Iran Air			1984	
19668	N93102	Trans World Airlines	131	12/7/69	12/31/69	
	5-282	Imp Iranian AF			11/14/75	
	5-8106	IIAF	131F		11/14/75	converted
	5-8106	Iranian Air Force			2/78	
	EP-NHD	Iran Air			4/83	
19669	N93103	Trans World Airlines	131	12/5/69	12/31/69	
	5-287	IIAF			12/12/75	
	5-8108	IIAF			12/12/75	
	5-8108	Iranian Air Force			2/78	
	EP-NHK	Iran Air			4/83	

s/n	reg	carrier	series	ff	dd	remarks
19670	N93104	Trans World Airlines	131		2/20/70	
19671	N93105	Trans World Airlines	131		3/9/70	
19672	N93106	Trans World Airlines	131		4/3/70	
19673	N93107	Trans World Airlines	131		4/29/70	
19674	N93108	Trans World Airlines	131		5/5/70	
19675	N93019	Trans World Airlines	131		5/23/70	
19676	N53110	Trans World Airlines	131		8/10/70	
19677	N53111	Trans World Airlines	131		9/26/70	
	5-283	IIAF			10/15/75	
	5-8104	IIAF	131F		10/15/75	converted w/o 5/9/76 Madrid, Spain
19678	N53112	Trans World Airlines	131		10/4/70	
	5-281	IIAF			3/15/75	
	5-8102	IIAF	131F		8/75	converted
	5-8102	IAF			2/78	
	EP-NHT	Iran Air			6/84	
19725	JA8101	Japan Air Lines	146		4/22/70	
19726	JA8102	Japan Air Lines	146		5/28/70	
	JA8102	Japan Asia			12/82	
19727	JA8103	Japan Air Lines	146		6/27/70	
	JA8103	Japan Asia			11/82	
19729	I-DEMA	Alitalia	143		5/13/70	*Niel Armstrong*
	N355AS	Boeing			11/3/81	
	N355AS	Hawaii Express			8/12/82	leased
	N355AS	Boeing			5/13/83	
	N355AS	Metro International			6/8/83	leased
	N355AS	Boeing			10/18/83	
	N603PE	People Express			6/27/84	leased
	N355AS	Boeing			1986	
	N17010	Continental			1988	
19730	N1796B	Boeing	143			
	I-DEME	Alitalia			7/1/70	*Arturo Ferrarin*
	I-DEME	Aer Lingus			9/26/76	leased
	I-DEME	Alitalia			10/17/76	
	N356AS	Boeing			9/17/81	
	N356AS	SAS			7/26/82	leased
	N356AS	Scanair			7/26/82	sub-leased
	N356AS	Icelandair			9/9/82	sub-leased
	N356AS	Air Algerie			9/9/82	sub-leased
	N356AS	Icelandair			10/25/82	
	N356AS	Scanair			10/25/82	
	N356AS	SAS			1982	
	N356AS	Boeing			12/9/82	
	N356AS	Overseas National			7/29/83	leased
	N356AS	Boeing			10/24/83	
	N356AS	Pakistan International			1984	leased
	N356AS	Boeing			10/3/84	WFU
	N606PE	People Express			6/17/85	
	N356AS	Boeing			1986	
	N17011	Continental			1988	
19731	I-DEMO	Alitalia	243B		3/9/71	*Francesco de Piredo*
	N357AS	Boeing			12/10/81	
	N357AS	Cargolux			8/17/83	leased
	N357AS	Boeing			10/28/83	
	N604PE	People Express			6/6/84	leased
	N604PE	Boeing			3/86	

s/n	reg	carrier	series	ff	dd	remarks
	N604PE	Integrated Aircraft Inc.		3/86		
	N604PE	People Express			3/86	leased
	N16020	Continental			1988	
19732	I-DEMU	Alitalia	243B		5/27/71	*Geo Chavez*
	N358AS	Boeing			11/19/81	
	N358AS	Overseas National			8/1/83	
	N358AS	Boeing			10/83	
	N358AS	National			1984	leased
	N358AS	Boeing			2/25/85	
	N611PE	People Express			2/30/85	
	B-2440	CAAC			5/20/85	leased
	N747BL	Boeing			12/18/85	
	G-VGIN	Virgin Air			5/31/86	
19733	N26861	Continental Airlines	124		5/18/70	
	5-289	IIAF			9/22/75	
	5-8110	IIAF	124F		9/75	converted
	N26861	Beoing			1/6/78	
	N750WA	World Airways			2/9/78	
	N809FT	Flying Tiger Line			7/1/78	leased
	N750WA	World Airways			7/15/80	
	N750WA	Flying Tiger Line			11/25/81	leased
	N750WA	World Airways			12/22/81	
	HK-2900	Avianca			7/2/82	leased
19734	N26862	Continental Airlines	124		7/13/70	
	5-290	IIAF			10/15/75	
	5-8111	IIAF			1976	
	N747AV	Boeing			9/76	
	HK-2000	Avianca			11/76	leased
	N747BA	Boeing			1/31/83	
	N747BA	SAS			8/14/83	leased
	N747BA	Air Algerie			8/14/83	sub-leased
	N747BA	SAS			10/20/83	
	N747BA	Boeing			10/20/83	
	N747BA	Avianca			12/15/83	leased
	N747BA	Boeing			1/14/84	
	N747BA	Tower Air			5/31/84	leased
	N602FF	Tower Air			1/86	
19735	N26863	Continental Airlines	124		8/12/70	
	5-291	IIAF			10/30/75	
	5-8112	IIAF	124F		10/75	converted
	N8389V	Boeing			4/11/77	
	4X-AXZ	El Al			6/21/77	
	HK-2400	Avianca			7/21/81	leased
	4X-AXZ	El Al			7/82	
	4X-AXZ	Cargo Airlines				leased
19744	EI-ASI	Aer Lingus	148		12/15/70	*St. Colmcille*
	HS-VGB	Air Siam			9/28/73	leased,*Doi Suthep*
	EI-ASI	Aer Lingus			4/17/76	*St. Colmcille*
	EI-ASI	Air Algerie			10/4/79	leased
	EI-ASI	Aer Lingus			10/13/79	*St. Patrick*
19745	EI-ASJ	Aer Lingus	148	3/4/71	3/18/71	
	EI-AJS	East African Airways			12/13/74	leased
	HS-VGF	Air Siam			4/19/75	leased
	EI-ASJ	Aer Lingus			5/15/75	*St. Patrick*
	G-BDPZ	British Airways			3/31/76	
	G-BDPZ	Aer Lingus			10/78	*St. Patrick*

s/n	reg	carrier	series	ff	dd	remarks
	G-BDPZ	British Caledonian			10/28/78	leased
	G-BDPZ	Aer Lingus			2/2/79	*St. Colmcille*
	G-BDPZ	BritishAirways			4/1/79	leased
	EI-ASJ	Aer Lingus			5/12/81	*St. Colmcille*
19746	N1800B	Boeing	130	2/18/70		
	D-ABYA	Lufthansa			5/10/70	*Nordhein-Westfalen*
	N610BN	ITEL			11/78	
	N610BN	Braniff			11/78	leased
	N610BN	ITEL			12/80	
	N610BN	GTAX Leasing			12/80	
	N610BN	Guinness Peat Aviation		12/80		
	N610BN	Braniff			12/80	leased
	N610BN	GTAX Leasing			10/23/81	
	N480GX	Viasa			1982	leased
	N480GX	GTAX Leasing			9/30/82	
	N480GX	Overseas National			5/8/83	
	N480GX	Egyptair			5/8/83	sub-leased
	N480GX	Overseas National			12/83	leased
	N480GX	GTAX Leasing			5/21/84	
	N780T	Transamerica			6/1/84	leased
	N780T	GTAX Leasing			11/8/85	
	N603FF	Tower Air			11/22/85	leased
19747	D-ABYB	Lufthansa	130		4/13/70	w/o 11/20/74 Narobi *Hassen*
19748	D-ABYC	Lufthansa	130		5/23/70	*Bayeon*
	D-ABYC	ITEL			1/79	
	EI-BED	Aer Lingus			1/3/70	leased, *St. Kieran*
	EI-BED	Air Algerie			10/15/79	sub-leased
	EI-BED	Aer LIngus			3/31/80	*St. Kieran*
	EI-BED	ITEL			12/80	
	EI-BED	GTAX Leasing			12/80	
	EI-BED	Aer LIngus			12/80	*St. Kieran*
	EI-BED	Air Jamaca			1982	leased
	EI-BED	Aer LIngus			1983	
19749	F-BPVA	Air France	128		3/20/70	
	F-BPVA	Alitalia			2/76	film *La Bonne Annee*
	F-BPVA	Air France			2/76	
19750	F-BVPB	Air France	128		3/25/70	
19751	F-BVPC	Air France	128		5/12/70	
19752	F-BVPD	Air France/Air Inter	128		7/14/70	week days/week-ends
19753	N4703U	United Airlines	122		6/30/70	*William M. Allen*
	N4703U	General Electric Corp			6/26/85	
	N4803U	Pan American			12/85	
19754	N4704U	United Airlines	122		8/4/70	
	N4704U	General Electric Corp			8/3/85	
	N4704U	Pan American			12/85	
19755	N4701U	United Airlines	122		12/28/70	
	N4701U	General Electric Corp			8/7/85	
	N4701U	Panm American			12/85	
19756	N4711U	United Airlines	122	8/18/70	8/31/70	
	N4711U	General Electric Corp			8/27/85	
	N4711U	Pan American			12/85	
19757	N4712U	United Airlines	122		8/70	
	N4712U	General Electric Corp			8/30/85	
	N4712U	Pan American			12/85	
19761	N1799B	Boeing	136	3/15/70		

s/n	reg	carrier	series	ff	dd	remarks
	G-AWNA	BOAC			5/23/70	
	G-AWNA	British Airways			4/1/72	*Colliford Lake*
19762	G-AWNB	BOAC	136		5/22/70	
	G-AWNB	British Airways			4/1/72	*Langorse Lake*
19763	G-AWNC	BOAC	136		6/29/70	
	G-AWNC	British Airways			4/1/72	*City of Belfast*
19764	G-AWND	BOAC	136	1/20/71	2/28/71	
	G-AWND	British Airways			4/1/72	*Christopher Marlowe*
19765	G-AWNE	BOAC	136	2/10/71	3/5/71	
	G-AWNE	British Airways			4/1/72	*Derwent Lake*
19766	G-AWNF	BOAC	136	2/13/71	3/14/71	
	G-AWNF	British Airways			4/1/72	*City of Westminster*
19778	N601US	Northwest Orient	151		4/30/70	
19799	N602US	Northwest Orient	151		5/12/70	
19780	N603US	Northwest Orient	151		5/22/70	
19781	N604US	Northwest Orient	151		6/24/70	
19782	N605US	Northwest Orient	151		6/24/70	
19783	N606US	Northwest Orient	151	8/22/70	8/30/70	
19784	N607US	Northwest Orient	151		9/9/70	
19785	N608US	Northwest Orient	151		9/12/70	
19786	N609US	Northwest Orient	151		10/28/70	
19787	N610US	Northwest Orient	151	1/6/70	11/11/70	
	N610US	Boeing			11/11/70	leased, sales tour
	N610US	Northwest Orient			1971	
19823	JA8104	Japan Airlines	246B		2/11/71	
19824	JA8105	Japan Airlines	246B	2/12/71	3/1/71	
19825	JA8106	Japan Airlines	246B	4/29/71	5/14/71	
19875	N4713U	United Airlines	122		11/3/70	damaged HNL 2/24/89
19876	N4714U	United Airlines	122		11/28/70	*Justin Dart*
19877	N4716U	United Airlines	122		12/12/70	
19878	N4717U	United Airlines	122		12/28/70	*Richard E. Carlson*
19879	N4718U	United Airlines	122	5/16/71	5/27/71	*Thomas F. Gleed*
19880	N4719U	United Airlines	122	7/15/71	6/26/71	*Friendship Japan*
19881	M4720U	United Airlines	122	7/13/71	7/23/71	
19882	N4723U	United Airlines	122	12/17/71	1/6/72	*William A. Patterson*
19883	N4727U	United Airlines	122	6/16/72	6/27/72	*Robert E. Johnson*
19896	N9896	Delta Air LInes	132		9/16/70	
	N9896	Boeing			9/16/74	
	LV-LRG	Aerolineas Argentina				NTU
	N4010B	Boeing			1976	
	B-1868	China Airlines			6/15/76	leased
	N902PA	Boeing			4/28/78	
	N902PA	Pan American			5/9/78	
19897	N9897	Delta Air LInes	132		10/22/70	
	N9897	Boeing			2/1/77	
	N803FT	Flying Tigers	132F		7/1/77	converted
	N803FT	Pan American				leased
	N803FT	Flying Tigers			1979	
	N803FT	Cargo Airlines			1979	leased
	N803FT	Flying Tigers			1979	
	N803FT	Cargo Airlines			12/17/79	leased
	N803FT	Flying Tigers			1/25/80	
19898	N9898	Delta Air Lines	132		11/18/70	
	N9898	Boeing			3/11/75	
	B-1860	China Airlines			5/16/75	
	N9898	Braniff Airlines			1979	leased

s/n	reg	carrier	series	ff	dd	remarks
	B-1860	China airlines			1979	
	EI-BOS	Guinness Peat			5/1/84	
	N725PA	Pan American			5/1/84	
19918	N77772	National Airlines	135		9/8/70	*Patricia; Jacquelyn*
	N620US	Northwest Orient			5/76	
19919	N77773	National Airlines	135		10/20/70	*Elizabeth; Linda*
	N621US	Northwest Orient			5/76	
19922	PH-BUA	KLM	206B		1/16/71	*Mississippi*
19923	PH-BUB	KLM	206B	2/15/71	3/4/71	*Danube*
19924	PH-BUC	KLM	206B	5/9/71	5/21/71	*Amazone*
19925	N4728U	United Airlines	122	1/22/73	4/27/73	*Gardner Crowles*
19926	N4729U	United Airlines	122	1/30/73	4/24/73	
19927	N4732U	United Airlines	122	2/14/73	3/19/73	
19928	N4735U	United Airlines	122	5/16/73	5/20/73	
19957	EC-BRO	Iberia	156		10/2/70	*Cervantes*
	N133TW	Trans World Airlines			5/1/80	
19958	EC-BRP	Iberia	156		11/10/70	*Lope de Vega*
	N134TW	Trans World airlines			3/17/81	
19959	VT-EBD	Air India	237B	3/8/71	3/22/71	*Emperor Ashoka* w/o 1/1/78 Bombay
19960	VT-EBE	Air India	237B	4/2/71	4/20/71	*Emperor Shahjehan*
20009	VH-EBA	Qantas	238B	7/8/71	7/30/71	*City of Canberra*
	VH-EBA	Air New Zeland			2/84	leased
	VH-EBA	Qantas			3/84	*City of Canberra*
	4R-ULF	Guinness Peat Aviation		6/8/84		
	4R-ULF	Air Lanka			6/8/84	leased
20010	VH-EBB	Qantas	238B	7/23/71	8/14/71	*City of Melbourne*
	VH-EBB	Guinness Peat Aviation		7/10/84		
	VH-EBB	Qantas			7/10/84	leased, *City of Melbourne*
	VH-EBB	Guinness Peat Aviation		10/23/85		
	4R-ULG	Air Lanka			10/30/85	leased
20011	VH-EBC	Qantas	238B	10/7/71	10/21/71	*City of Sidney*
	N747BM	Boeing			12/3/84	
	N607PE	People Express			4/15/85	
	N50022	Continental			1988	
20012	VH-EBD	Qantas	238B	11/23/71	12/8/71	*City of Perth*
	N371EA	Eastern Air Lines				NTU
	N747BN	Boeing			3/85	
	N608PE	People Express			9/27/85	
	N10023	Continental			1988	
20013	CF-TOA	Air Canada	133		2/11/71	
	C-FTOA	Global International			6/1/83	leased
	C-FTOA	Air Canada			9/83	
	C-FTOA	Guinness Peat Aviation		7/28/84		
	N749R	National Airlines			7/28/84	leased
	N749R	Malaysian Airline System			12/84	sub-leased
	N749R	National Airlines			10/8/84	leased
	EI-BPH	Guinness Peat Aviation		10/8/84		
	EI-BPH	People Express			2/12/85	leased
	EI-BPH	Guinness Peat Aviation		5/1/85		
	EI-BPH	Middle Eastern Airlines			6/26/85	leased
	EI-BPH	Guinness Peat Aviation		9/22/85		
	EI-BPH	Flying Tigers			9/22/85	leased
20014	CF-TOB	Air Canada	133	3/1/71	3/18/71	
	CF-TOB	Guinness Peat Aviation		5/2/85		
	EC-DXE	Iberia			5/3/85	leased

s/n	reg	carrier	series	ff	dd	remarks
	EC-DXE	Aviaco			5/3/85	sub-leased
	EI-BRR	Guinness Peat Aviation		11/1/85		
	EI-BRR	Middle East Airlines			5/30/86	leased
	EI-BRR	Olympic Airways			6/68	sub-leased
	EI-BRR	Middle East Airlines			6/86	leased
	EI-BRR	Egyptair			6/27/86	sub-leased
	EI-BRR	Middle Ease Airlines			6/30/86	leased
20015	CF-TOC	Air Canada	133	6/11/71	6/24/71	
	CF-TOC	Royal Air Maroc			9/1/82	leased
	CF-TOC	Air Canada			9/22/82	
	CF-TOC	Royal Air Maroc			10/1/82	leased
	CF-TOC	Air Canada			10/23/82	
	C-FTOC	Royal Air Maroc			9/1/83	leased
	C-FTOC	Air Canada			10/83	
20080	N7401Q	Eastern Airlines	125			NTU
	N93113	Trans World Airlines			10/22/70	
	5-282	IIAF			3/31/75	
	5-8103	IIAF	125F		10/3/75	converted
	5-8103	IAF			2/78	
	EP-NHS	Iran Air			1984	
20081	N7402Q	Eastern Airlines	125			NTU
	N93114	Trans World Airlines			11/2/70	
	5-284	IIAF			11/3/75	
	5-8105	IIAF			2/13/76	
	5-8102	IAF			2/78	
	EP-NHR	Iran Air			6/84	
20082	N7403Q	Eastern Airlines	125	8/4/71		NTU
	N93118	Trans World Airlines			9/29/71	
	5-286	IIAF			11/13/75	
	5-8107	IIAF	125F		1/14/76	converted
	5-8107	IAF			2/78	
	EP-NHP	Iran Air			6/84	
20083	N7404Q	Eastern Airlines	125	8/14/71		NTU
	N93119	Trans World Airlines			10/27/71	
	5-8109	IIAF			12/15/75	
	N93119	Trans World Airlines			12/15/76	
20100	N9661	American Airlines	123		6/18/70	
	N9661	Boeing	123F		2/13/74	converted
	N800FT	Flying Tiger Line			8/74	
	N903PA	Pan American			1/78	leased
	N800FT	Flying Tiger LIne			8/2/79	
	N9661	American Airlines			2/14/81	
	N9661	United Parcel Service			12/20/84	operated by Orion Air
	N674UP	United Parcel Service			1/85	operated by Orion Air
20101	N9662	American Airlines	123		7/16/70	
	N9662	Boeing	123F		2/14/74	converted
	N801FT	Flying Tiger Line			9/24/74	
	N801FT	Lufthansa			1/24/75	leased
	N801FT	Flying Tiger Line			3/1/75	
	N801FT	El Al			9/21/77	leased
	N801FT	Flying Tiger LIne			6/29/78	
	N662AA	American Airlines			2/25/80	leased
	N801FT	Flying Tiger LIne			4/19/80	
	N9676	American Airlines			6/81	
	N9676	United Parcel Service			12/18/84	operated by Orion Air
	N676UP	United Parcel Service			1/85	operated by Orion Air

s/n	reg	carrier	series	ff	dd	remarks
20102	N9663	American Airlines	123		6/30/70	
	N9663	Citicorp			6/6/84	
	N9663	National Airlines			6/6/84	leased
	N9663	Dominica			5/85	leased
	N9663	National Airlines			1985	leased
	N9663	Citicorp			11/21/85	
	N9663	Jet 24 Int'l Airways			3/14/86	leased
	N14943	Citicorp			6/86	
	N14943	Cargolux			1/19/86	leased
20103	N9664	American Airlines	123		8/27/70	
	N9664	Citicorp			5/20/84	
	N9664	Avianca			5/20/84	leased
20104	N9665	American Airlines	123		9/18/70	
	N9665	Citicorp			5/2/84	
	N9665	American Airlines			5/2/84	
	N9665	Citicorp			1984	
	N9665	Dominica			4/20/85	leased
	HI-472	Dominica			1/86	leased
20105	N9666	American Airlines	123		10/2/70	
	N9666	Braniff			3/1/78	leased
	N9666	American Airlines			3/31/80	
	N9666	Citicorp			6/15/84	
	N9666	National Airlines			6/15/84	leased
	N9666	Citicorp			9/85	
	N14936	Cargolux			6/19/86	leased
20106	N9667	American Airlines	123		10/8/70	
	N9667	Steven's Corporation				movie *Airport 77*
	N9667	American Airlines				
	N9667	Citicorp			5/30/84	
	N9667	National Airlines			7/23/84	leased
	N9667	Citicorp			5/20/85	
	N14937	Citicorp			6/86	
	LX-MCV	Cargolux			6/19/86	leased
20107	N9668	American Airlines	123		10/29/70	
	N905NA	NASA			6/18/74	*The Odd Couple*
20108	N9669	American Airlines	123		11/27/70	
	N9669	Citicorp			5/11/84	
	N9669	National Airlines			7/27/84	leased
	N9669	Citicorp			9/85	
	N14939	Cargolux			6/19/86	leased
20109	N9670	American Airlines	123		12/29/70	
	N9670	Citicorp			5/25/84	
	N9670	Pan American			5/29/84	
20116	HB-IGA	Swissair	257B		1/30/71	*Geneve*
	HB-IGA	Salenia			10/27/82	
	HB-IGA	Swissair			10/27/82	leased
	LX-SAL	Salenia			12/30/83	
	LX-SAL	Air National			3/2/84	
	LX-SAL	Salenia			1984	
	LX-SAL	National Airlines			3/27/85	leased
	LX-SAL	Egyptair			3/5/85	leased
	LX-SAL	National Airlines			5/85	leased
	LX-SAL	Salenia			5/85	
	N303TW	Trans World Airlines			5/85	
20117	HB-IGB	Swissair	257B	3/13/71	3/26/71	*Zurich*
	HB-IGB	Wihemsens			12/82	

s/n	reg	carrier	series	ff	dd	remarks
	HB-IGB	Swissair			12/82	leased
	HB-IGB	KANSA			2/84	stored Marana
	SU-GAK	National Airlines			5/15/84	leased
	SU-GAK	Egyptair			5/15/84	leased
	SU-GAK	National Airlines			2/25/85	leased
	SU-GAK	KANSA			2/25/85	
	N304TW	Trans World Airlines			3/26/85	
20120	SE-DDL	SAS	283B	2/6/71	3/11/71	*Ivar Viking*
	SE-DDL	Scanair			9/82	
	SE-DDL	SAS			3/83	
	SE-DDL	Air Invest			10/10/83	
	LN-AET	SAS			10/10/83	leased
	LN-AET	Air Invest			7/27/85	
	LN-AET	Gulf Air			7/27/85	leased
20121	OY-KFA	SAS	283B	10/28/71		NTU
	OH-KHA	SAS			11/20/71	*Huge Viking*
	LN-AEO	Air Invest			1/29/82	
	LN-AEO	SAS			1/29/82	leased
	LN-AEO	Nigeria Airways			4/1/82	leased
	LN-AEO	SAS			1/1/83	leased
	LN-AEO	Air Invest			3/3/86	
	G-BGMS	British Airtours			3/3/86	leased, *City of Swansea*
20135	4X-AXA	El Al	258B	3/15/71	3/26/71	
20137	EC-BRQ	Iberia	256B	12/9/71	1/4/72	
20207	N601BN	Braniff	127	1/5/71		WFU 5/12/82
	N601BN	Polaris Leasing			12/82	
	N601BN	Metro International			3/2/83	leased
	N601BN	Polaris Leasing			11/83	
	N601BN	Tower Air			11/83	leased
20208	N602BN	Braniff	127	3/25/71		NTU
	N800U	Universal Airlines				NTU
	C-FDJC	Wardair	1D1		4/23/73	*Phil Garratt*
20235	N7470	Boeing	121	2/9/69		prototype
	N1352B	Boeing			7/1/70	demonstrator
20237	N1795B	Boeing	244B	8/25/71		
	ZS-SAL	South African A'ways			1/26/72	*Tafelburg*
20238	ZS-SAM	South African A'ways	244B	12/5/71	12/13/71	*Drakensburg*
20239	ZS-SAN	South African A'ways	244B	9/30/71	10/22/71	*Lebombo*
20246	N9899	Delta Airlines	132		9/30/71	
	N9899	Boeing			3/77	
	N804FT	Flying Tigers			3/24/77	converted
	N804FT	Cargo Airlines			12/16/79	leased
	N804FT	Flying Tigers			3/27/80	
20247	N9900	Delta Airlines	132		11/11/71	
	N9900	Boeing			4/77	
	N805FT	Flying Tigers	132F		5/6/77	converted
20269	G-AWNG	BOAC	136	7/30/71	9/8/71	
	G-AWNG	British Airways			4/1/72	
20270	G-AWNH	BOAC	136	11/9/71	11/23/71	*City of London*
	G-AWNH	British Airways			4/1/72	
20271	G-AWNI	BOAC	136	12/3/71	1/7/72	*Sir Walter Raleigh*
	G-AWNI	British Airways			4/1/72	
	N17125	Trans World Airlines			3/25/81	
20272	G-AWNJ	BOAC	136	3/6/72	3/21/72	
	G-AWNJ	British Airways			4/1/72	*Brassenthwaite Water*

s/n	reg	carrier	series	ff	dd	remarks
20273	G-AWNK	BOAC	136	3/10/72	3/24/72	
	G-AWNK	British Airways			4/1/72	
	N17126	Trans World Airlines			3/30/81	
20274	4X-AXB	El Al	258B	10/29/71	11/22/71	
20284	G-AWNL	British Airways	136	4/4/72	4/19/72	*Emerdale Water*
20305	N26864	Continental Airlines	124	6/18/71	6/25/71	*Robert F. Six*
	C-FFUN	Wardair	1D1		12/15/74	*Romeo Vachon*
20320	N93115	Trans World Airlines	131	12/22/70	5/20/71	
	N93115	GTAX Leasing			6/84	
	N472EV	Evergreen Int'al	131F		3/86	converted
20321	N53116	Trans World Airlines	131	5/7/71	5/22/71	
	N53116	GTAX Leasing			6/86	
20323	N9671	American Airlines	123	2/10/71	2/26/71	
	N9671	Boeing			3/75	
	N802FT	Flying Tigers	123F/SC		7/22/75	converted
	N802FT	American Airlines			2/81	leased
	N9671	American Airlines			5/81	
	N9671	United Parcel Service			11/13/84	operated by Orion Air
	N671UP	United Parcel Service			1/85	operated by Orion Air
20324	N9672	American Airlines	123	3/17/71	4/16/71	
	N9672	American Airlines	123F		4/12/76	converted
	N9672	United Parcel Service			10/2/84	operated by Orion Air
	N672UP	United Parcel Service			1/85	operated by Orion Air
20325	N9673	American Airlines	123	3/31/71	4/20/71	
	N9673	American Airlines	123F		7/76	converted
	N9673	El Al			10/78	leased
	N9673	American Airlines			11/78	
	N9673	United Parcel Service			8/28/84	operated by Orion Air
	N673UP	United Parcel Service			1/85	operated by Orion Air
20326	N9674	American Airlines	123	4/23/71	5/12/71	
	N9674	Pan American			12/1/83	
20332	JA8107	Japan Airlines	246B	10/4/71	10/28/71	
	JA8107	Japan Airlines	246SCD		9/77	converted
20333	JA8108	Japan Airlines	246B	10/25/71	11/30/71	
20347	N652PA	Pan American	121	12/17/70	4/25/71	*Clipper Pacific Trader*
20348	N653PA	Pan American	121	12/31/70	4/8/71	*Clipper Unity*
	N653PA	Pan American	121/SCD		3/77	converted
20349	N654PA	Pan American	121	4/14/71	4/27/71	*Clipper White King*
	N654PA	Pan American	121/SCD		3/77	converted
	N817FT	Flying Tigers			2/24/83	
20350	N655PA	Pan American	121	5/3/71	5/28/71	*Clipper Wild Fire*
	N655PA	Pan American	121/SCD		4/15/75	converted
20351	N656PA	Pan American	121	5/21/71	6/18/71	*Clipper Live Yankee*
	N656PA	Evergreen			1988	leased
20352	N657PA	Pan American	121	5/27/71	6/19/71	*Clipper Artic*
	N657PA	Evergreen			1988	leased
20353	N658PA	Pan American	121	6/2/71		*Clipper High Flyer*
	N658PA	Pan American	121/SCD		7/2/76	converted
	N818FT	Flying Tigers			2/24/83	
20354	N659PA	Pan American	121	7/9/71		*Clipper Plymouth Rock*
	N659PA	Pan American			12/19/73	leased
	N659PA	Iran Air			11/20/74	leased
	N659PA	Pan American			1/18/75	
20355	F-BPVE	Air France	128	2/2/71	3/16/71	
20356	N611US	Northwest Orient	251B	10/11/70	3/26/71	
20357	N612US	Northwest Orient	251B	5/5/71	5/16/71	

s/n	reg	carrier	series	ff	dd	remarks
20358	N613US	Northwest Orient	251B	6/4/71	6/22/71	
20359	N614US	Northwest Orient	251B	10/22/71	11/15/71	
20360	N615US	Northwest Orient	251B	11/13/71	11/23/71	
20372	D-ABYD	Lufthansa	230B	4/16/71	5/5/71	*Baden-Wurrtemburg*
	D-ABYD	ITEL			11/26/78	
	HL7440	Korean Airlines			12/9/78	leased
	HL7440	ITEL			12/80	
	HL7440	GTAX Boothe			12/80	
	HL7440	Korean Airlines			12/80	leased
20373	N1794B	Boeing	230F	11/30/71		
	D-ABYE	Lufthansa			3/31/72	
	D-ABYE	ITEL			12/15/78	
	HL7441	Korean Airlines			12/15/78	leased
	HL7441	ITEL			12/80	
	HL7441	GTAX Boothe			12/80	
	HL7441	Korean Airlines			12/80	leased
20376	F-BPVF	Air France	128		2/4/72	
20377	F-BPVG	Air France	128		2/2/72	
20378	F-BPVH	Air France	128		3/1/72	
20390	N9675	American Airlines	123	5/7/71	5/25/71	
	N9675	Columbia Airways			9/74	for movie *Airport 75*
	N9675	American Airlines	123F		12/74	converted
	OD-AGM	TMA			6/1/76	leased
	N9675	American Airlines			1/8/77	
	N9675	United Parcel Service			9/12/84	operated by Orion Air
	N675UP	United Parcel Service			1/85	operated by Orion Air
20391	N9676	American Airlines	123	6/11/71	6/25/71	
	N9676	American Airlines	123F		10/31/74	converted
	N9676	TMA			5/15/75	leased
	OD-AGC	TMA			9/12/75	
	N901PA	Pan American			6/28/77	
	N820FT	Flying Tigers			2/24/83	
20398	PH-BUD	KLM	206B	8/6/72	8/31/71	*The Nile*
	PH-BUD	Kenya Airways			11/7/80	leased
	PH-BUD	KLM			4/20/81	
20399	PH-BUE	KLM	206B	9/3/71	9/30/71	*The Rio de la Plata*
	HS-VGG	Air Siam			4/16/76	leased
	PH-BUE	KLM			1/19/77	
20400	PH-BUF	KLM	206B	9/14/71	10/19/71	*The Rhine* w/o 3/27/77 Tenerife
20401	OO-SGA	Sabena	129		11/19/70	
	OO-SGA	Sabena	129A		2/15/74	converted
20402	OO-SGB	Sabena	129		12/4/70	
	OO-SGB	Sabena	129A		4/1/74	converted
20427	PH-BUG	KLM	206B	11/22/71	12/15/71	*The Orinoco*
	PH-BUG	Via/KLM			2/15/72	Stbd/Port
	PH-BUG	KLM			6/1/74	
20459	VT-EBN	Air India	237B		3/72	*Emperor Rajendra Chola*
20493	D-ABYF	Condor	230B	3/17/71	4/20/71	*Fritz*
	HL7447	ITEL			6/18/79	
	HL7447	Korean Airlines			6/22/79	leased
	HL7447	Saudia			6/22/79	leased
	HL7447	Korean Airlines			12/79	leased
	HL7447	Saudia			11/1/80	leased
	HL7447	Korean Airlines			11/30/80	leased
	HL7447	ITEL			12/80	

s/n	reg	carrier	series	ff	dd	remarks
	HL7447	GTAX/Boothe			12/80	
	HL7447	Korean Airlines			12/80	leased
20501	CS-TJA	TAP Air Portugal	282B		2/16/72	*Portugal*
	N301TW	Trans World Airlines			6/4/84	
20502	CS-TJB	TAB Air Protugal	282B	5/4/72	5/16/72	*Brasil*
	N302TW	Trans World Airlines			10/30/84	
20503	JA8109	Japan Airlines	246B		3/2/72	hijacked Paris 7/20/73 blown-up Benghazi w/o 7/23/73
20504	JA8110	Japan Airlines	246B		3/13/72	
20505	JA8111	Japan Airlines	246B	3/3/72	3/21/72	
20520	I-DEMB	Alitalia	243B		3/26/72	*Carlo de Prete*
	N45224	Boeing			12/10/80	
	N359AS	Boeing			12/12/80	
	N359AS	Cargolux			8/24/82	leased
	N359AS	Kabo Air			8/24/82	leased
	N359AS	Cargolux			1982	leased
	N359AS	Boeing			11/22/82	
	N359AS	Overseas National			6/14/83	leased
	N359AS	Boeing			11/8/83	leased
	N605PE	People Express			6/15/84	leased
	N605PE	People Express			12/20/84	
	N33021	Continental			1988	
20527	D-ABYG	Lufthansa	230B	2/9/72	2/25/72	*Niedersachsen*
	D-ABYG	ITEL			5/3/79	
	N611BN	Braniff			3/3/79	leased
	N611BN	GTAX/Boothe			4/14/82	
	N611BN	Chemco Leasing			4/14/82	
	G-BJXN	British Caledonian			4/14/82	leased
20528	JA8112	Japan Airlines	246B	5/26/72	6/14/72	
20529	JA8113	Japan Airlines	246B	6/9/72	6/29/72	
20530	N1800B	Boeing	246B	8/23/72		
	JA8114	Japan Airlines			11/3/72	
20531	JA8115	Japan Airlines	246B	8/18/72	10/4/782	
20532	JA8116	Japan Airlines	246B	10/6/72	12/8/72	
20534	VH-EBE	Qantas Airlines	238B	7/27/72	8/10/73	*City of Brisbane*
	VH-EBE	Boeing			6/85	
	VH-EBE	Qantas Airlines			6/85	leased
	VH-EBE	Boeing			1/31/86	
	N609PE	People Express			5/1/86	
	N10024	Continental			1988	
20535	VH-EBF	Qantas	238B	7/13/72	8/1/72	*City of Adelaide*
	VH-EBF	Boeing			11/85	
	VH-EBF	Qantas			11/85	leased
	VH-EBF	Boeing			2/28/86	
	N610PE	People Express			7/86	
	N17025	Continental			1988	
20541	N28903	Wilmington Trust Co.	128	10/26/72		
	N28903	Air France			2/21/73	leased
	F-BPVJ	Air France			12/29/81	
20542	N28888	Wilmington Trust Co.	128	10/30/72		
	N28888	Air France			3/21/73	leased w/o 6/12/75 Bombay after 6 hour fire
20543	N28889	Wilmington Trust Co.	128	12/15/72		
	N28889	Air France			3/31/73	leased

s/n	reg	carrier	series	ff	dd	remarks
	F-BPVK	Air France			12/29/81	
20556	ZS-SAO	South African Airways	244B	6/14/72	8/7/72	*Magaliesberg*
20557	ZS-SAP	South African Airways	244B	9/15/72	9/29/72	*Swartberg*
20558	VT-EBO	Air India	237B	4/14/72	6/1/72	*Emperor Niknamaditya*
20559	D-ABYH	Condor	230B	3/17/72	4/7/72	*Max*
	D-ABYH	ITEL			2/7/79	
	HL7442	Korean Airlines			2/7/79	leased
						w/o 9/1/83 Hokkaido
20651	N747WA	Greyhound Leasing	273C	3/23/72	4/27/72	
	N747WA	World Airways			4/27/72	leased
	N535PA	Pan American Cargo			10/20/74	leased, *Clipper Mercury*
	N747WR	World Airways			12/21/79	leased
	N747WR	Air Algerie			4/2/80	leased
	N747WR	World Airways			3/31/81	leased
	N747WR	Malaysian Airline System		1982		leased
	N747WR	World Airways			1982	leased
	N747WR	Visia			12/6/82	leased
	N747WR	World Airways			1/31/83	leased
	N747WR	Greyhound Leasing			10/83	
	N747WR	National Airlines			11/17/83	
	N747WR	Evergreen International		3/16/85		
	N747WR	Flying Tigers			3/16/85	leased
	N747WR	Evergreen International		3/1/86		
	N747WR	Air India			3/1/86	leased
	N747WR	Evergreen International		3/1/87		
20652	N748WA	Greyhound Leasing	273C	4/25/72	5/25/72	
	N748WA	World Airways			5/25/72	leased
	N748WA	Air Algerie			11/12/75	leased
	N748WA	World Airways			1/11/76	leased
	N748WA	El Al			1/77	leased
	N748WA	World Airways			3/13/77	leased
	N748WA	Air Algerie			11/1/78	leased, Air Niger logos
	N748WA	World Airways			12/6/78	leased
	N748WA	Seaboard World			10/1/78	leased
	N748WA	Flying Tigers			10/1/80	leased
	N748WA	World Airways			10/5/80	leased
	N748WA	Malaysian Airline System			1982	leased
	N748WA	World Airways			1982	leased
	N748WA	Metro International			2/24/83	leased
	N748WA	World Airways			11/5/83	leased
	N748WA	Greyhound Leasing			11/5/83	leased
	N748WA	National Airlines			11/5/83	
	N748WA	Flying Tigers			11/5/83	leased
	N748WA	National Airlines			1984	
	N748WA	American Airlines			1984	leased
	N748WA	National Airlines			1984	
	N748WA	Flying Tigers			1984	leased
	N748WA	National Airlines			4/15/85	
	HL7471	Korean Airlines			4/15/85	leased
	HL7471	Saudia			5/8/85	leased
	HL7471	Korean Air			8/12/85	
	HL7471	Saudia			8/12/85	leased
	HL7471	Korean Air			5/27/86	
20653	N749WA	World Airways	273C	5/2/74	6/10/74	
	N749WA	Korean Air			6/11/74	leased
	N749WA	World Airways			3/20/79	

s/n	reg	carrier	series	ff	dd	remarks
	N749WA	Braniff			4/10/79	leased
	N749WA	World Airways			6/9/81	
	N749WA	Visia			6/15/81	leased
	N749WA	World Airways			6/81	
	N749WA	Lufthansa			10/27/83	leased
	N749WA	World Airways			4/4/84	leased
	N749WA	American Airlines			4/15/84	leased
	N749WA	World Airways			1984	
	N749WA	Flying Tigers			10/10/84	leased
	N749WA	Evergreen International			10/10/86	leased
20682	73-01676	United States Air Force	E4A	6/13/73	6/16/73	
20683	73-01677	United States Air Force	E4A	9/11/73	10/3/73	
20684	73-00787	United States Air Force	E4A	6/6/74	10/15/74	
20704	N1799B	Boeing	258B	4/5/73		
	4X-AXC	El Al			4/18/73	
20708	G-AWNM	British Airways	136	4/6/73	5/3/73	*Ullswater*
20712	9V-SIA	Singapore Airlines	212B	7/13/73	7/31/73	
	N747TA	Tigerair		12/8/79		
	N747TA	Flying Tiger Line			12/8/79	
	N747TA	Metro International			2/81	leased
	N747FT	Metro International			4/16/82	leased
	N747FT	Flying Tiger Line			2/24/83	
	N747FT	Pan American			2/24/83	
	N747FT	Metro International			2/24/83	leased
	N728PA	Pan American			3/25/83	
20713	9V-SIB	Singapore	212B	8/1/73	8/29/73	
	N748TA	Tigerair			7/31/80	
	N748TA	Flying Tiger Line			8/80	
	N748TA	Metro International			2/81	leased
	N748FT	Metro International			4/9/82	leased
	N748FT	Flying Tiger			2/24/83	
	N729PA	Pan American			2/24/83	
20742	SX-OAA	Olympic Airways	284B	6/2/73	6/21/76	*Olympic Zeus*
	N305TW	Trans World Airways			4/11/85	
20767	C-FTOD	Air Canada	133	5/3/73	5/14/73	
20770	N1798B	Boeing	2B5B	4/16/73		
	HL7410	Korean Airlines			5/1/73	
	N747BA	Boeing			4/15/81	
	HL7463	Orient Leasing			7/26/62	
	HL7463	Korean Airlines			7/27/82	leased
20771	N1796B	Boeing	2B5B			
	HL7411	Korean Airlines			7/12/73	
	N747BC	Boeing			11/25/81	
	HL7464	Orient Leasing			7/30/82	
	HL7464	Korean Airlines			7/27/82	leased
20781	N1795B	Boeing	SR46	8/31/73		
	JA8117	Japan Airlines			9/26/73	
20782	JA8118	Japan Airlines	SR46	12/10/73	12/21/73	
20783	JA8119	Japan Airlines	SR46	1/28/74	2/19/74	w/o 8/12/85 near Tokyo bulkhead failure
20784	JA8120	Japan Airlines	SR46	2/8/74	2/20/74	
20798	N88931	Wilmington Trust Co.	128	10/25/73		
	N88931	Air France			3/21/74	
	F-BPVL	Air France				
20799	N63305	Boeing	128	11/30/73		
	N63305	Air France			12/21/73	

s/n	reg	carrier	series	ff	dd	remarks
	F-BPVM	Air France			4/1/82	
20800	N28366	Wilmington Trust Co	128	1/10/74		
	N28366	Air France			2/8/74	
	F-BPVN	Air France			4/1/82	
20801	N1794B	Boeing	217B	11/2/73		
	C-FCRA	CP Air			11/15/73	Empress of Japan
	AP-BCN	Pakistan International			9/80	
20802	C-FCRB	CP Air	217B	11/15/73	12/3/73	Empress of Canada
	AP-BCM	Pakistan International			5/8/86	
20809	G-AWNN	British Airways	136	9/20/73	11/7/73	Lowes Water
20810	G-AWNO	British Airways	136	10/8/73	12/7/73	
20825	SX-OAB	Olympic Airways	284B	10/12/73	12/7/73	Olympic Eagle
20826	N701SW	Seaboard World	245F	7/12/74	7/31/74	
	N701SW	Visia				leased
	N701SW	Seaboard World			1980	
	N811FT	Flying Tiger			10/1/80	Huston Rehrig
20827	N702SW	Seaboard World	245F		4/30/76	
	N812FT	Flying Tiger			10/1/80	
20828	N703SW	Seaboard World				cancelled
20829	9Q-CKF	Air Zaire	198			cancelled
20841	VH-EBG	Qantas	238B	2/28/74	3/22/74	City of Hobart
20842	VH-EBH	Qantas	238B	3/13/74	3/24/74	City of Newcastle
20881	C-FTOE	Air Canada	133B	4/19/74	5/13/74	
20887	N18815	Wilmington Trust Co.	128F	9/11/74	10/4/74	
	N18815	Air France			10/4/74	
	F-BVPO	Air France			4/1/82	
20888	9V-SQC	Singapore Airlines	212B	6/21/74	7/29/74	
	N749TA	Tigerair			9/16/80	
	N749TA	Flying Tiger			9/16/80	
	N749TA	Metro International			2/81	leased
	N749FT	Pan American			2/24/83	leased
	N730PA	Pan American			3/6/83	
20921	VH-EBI	Qantas	238B	7/28/74	10/10/74	City of Darwin
20923	JA8121	Japan Airlines	SR46	3/14/74	3/28/74	
20924	JA8122	Japan Airlines	246B	3/21/74	3/29/74	
20927	C-FCRD	CP Air	217B	10/4/74	11/5/74	Empress of Australia
	N620BN	Braniff			11/15/78	
	C-FCRD	CP Air			12/6/78	
	AP-BCP	Pakistan International		10/86	scheduled	
20928	CS-TJC	TAP	282B	5/30/74	6/7/74	
	AP-AYV	Pakistan International			4/23/76	leased
	AP-AYV	Pakistan International			4/80	
20929	C-FCRE	CP Air	217B	11/15/74	12/2/74	Empress of Italy
	AP-BCL	Pakistan International			12/18/85	
20949	75-00125	USAF	E4B	4/29/75	4/4/75	
20952	G-AWNP	British Airways	126	9/20/74	11/6/74	Sir Jeff Hawkins
20953	G-BBPU	British Airways	136	10/22/74	3/15/75	Virginia Water
20954	F-BPVP	Air France	128	123/18/74	3/13/75	
	F-BPVP	Sabena			9/78	leased
20977	C-FTOF	Air Canada	233B/CO			NTU
	N8297V	Boeing				
	C-GAGA	Air Canada			3/7/75	
	C-GAGA	National			6/15/83	
	C-GAGA	Air Canada			11/83	
20998	EP-IAA	Iran Air	SP86	2/20/76	3/12/76	Fars
20999	EP-IAB	Iran Air	SP86	4/22/76	5/10/76	Kurdistan

s/n	reg	carrier	series	ff	dd	remarks
21022	N747SP	Boeing	SP21	7/4/75		
	N530PA	Pan American			4/26/76	*Clipper Mayflower*
	N140UA	United Airlines			2/11/86	
21023	N247SP	Boeing	SP21	8/14/75		
	N531PA	Pan American			5/17/76	*Clipper Freedom*
	N141UA	United Airlines			2/11/86	
21024	N342SP	Boeing	SP21	10/10/75		
	N532PA	Pan American			3/29/76	*Clipper Constitution*
	N142UA	United Airlines			2/11/86	
21025	N41035	Boeing	SP21	11/3/75		
	N533PA	Pan American			3/5/76	"Clipper Young America"
	N143UA	United Airlines			2/11/86	
21026	N534PA	Pan American	SP21	5/7/76	5/28/78	"Clipper Great Republic"
	N144UA	United Airlines			2/11/86	
21027	N535PA	Pan American	SP21			NTU
21028	N536PA	Pan American	SP21		1978	NTU
	N145UA	United Airlines			2/11/86	
21029	JA8128	Japan Airlines	146		6/20/75	
21030	JA8125	Japan Airlines	246B	12/5/74	12/17/74	
21031	JA8127	Japan Airlines	246B	2/10/75	5/12/75	
21032	JA8124	Japan Airlines	SR46	11/4/74	11/22/74	
21033	JA8126	Japan Airlines	SR46	1/24/75	4/2/75	
21034	JA8123	Japan Airlines	246F	8/2/74	9/17/74	
21035	CS-TJD	TAP	282B	2/27/75	10/27/75	
	AP-AYW	Pakistan International			4/13/75	leased
	AP-AYW	Pakistan International			4/80	
21048	9V-SQD	Singapore Airlines	212B	1/20/75	2/6/75	
	N747BC	Boeing			6/28/83	
	N747BC	Cargolux			1983	leased
	N747BC	Boeing			10/25/83	
	N747BC	Pan American			6/8/84	
	N747BC	Cargolux			8/18/83	leased
21054	VH-EBJ	Qantas	238B	4/21/75	5/30/75	*City of Geelong*
21079	OD-AGH	Middle East Airlines	2B46/CO	5/30/75	6/5/75	
	OD-AGH	Saudia			6/1/77	leased
	OD-AGH	Middle East Airlines			6/81	
	OD-AGH	Saudia			4/84	leased
	OD-AGH	Middle East Airlines			4/85	
	N202AE	CPC Leasing/AmEx			12/84	
	N202AE	Middle East Airlines			12/84	leased
	G-BLVE	British Airways			6/1/85	leased, *City of Lincoln*
21093	EP-IAC	Iran Air	SP86	5/16/77	7/25/77	*Khuzestan*
21098	OD-AGI	Middle East Airways	2B46/CO	6/5/75	6/20/75	
	OD-AGI	Saudia			6/1/77	leased
	OD-AGI	Middle East Airlines			6/81	
	OD-AGI	Gulf Air			3/27/84	leased
	N203AE	CPC Leasing/AmEx			12/15/84	
	N203AE	Middle East Airlines			12/15/84	leased
	N203AE	Gulf Air			12/15/84	leased
	N203AE	Middle EAst Airlines			8/85	leased, *City of Lancaster*
	G-BLVF	British Airways			11/85	leased
21099	OD-AGJ	Middle East Airlines	2B46/CO	8/7/75	8/20/75	
	OD-ADJ	Royal Air Maroc			1/77	leased (Tunis Air)
	OD-ADJ	Middle East Airlines			1977	
	OD-ADJ	Air Fance			6/1/77	leased
	OD-ADJ	Air Gabon			6/1/77	leased

s/n	reg	carrier	series	ff	dd	remarks
	OD-ADJ	Middle East Airlines			5/11/78	
	OD-AGJ	Saudia			9/78	leased
	OD-AGJ	Middle East Airlines			12/1/80	
	OD-ADJ	Saudia			2/81	leased
	N204AE	CPC Leasing/AmEx			5/85	
	N204AE	Middle East Airlines			5/85	leased
	N204AE	Egyptair			5/85	leased
	N204AE	Middle Ease Airlines			7/6/86	leased
21110	PH-BUH	KLM	206B/CO	9/26/75	10/19/75	Dr. Albert Plesman
21111	N8297V	Boeing	206B/CO	11/26/75		
	PH-BUI	KLM			12/16/75	Wilbur Wright
	PH-BUI	KLM	206B/SU		10/9/85	converted
21120	N616US	Northwest Orient	251F/SC	5/27/85	7/3/75	
21121	N617US	Northwest Orient	251F/SC	6/23/75	7/9/75	
21122	N618US	Northwest Orient	251F/SC	8/15/75	8/29/75	
21132	ZS-SPA	South African Airways	SP44	2/17/76	3/19/76	Matroosberg
	LX-LTM	Luxair			1980	NTU
	ZS-SPA	South African Airways			1980	
21133	ZS-SPB	South African Airways	SP44	3/10/76	4/22/76	Outeniqua
	7Q-YKL	Air Malawi			4/12/85	leased
	ZS-SPB	South African Airways			5/15/85	
21134	ZS-SPC	South African Airways	SP44	6/4/76	6/16/76	Maluti
	3B-NAG	Air Maraitius			10/28/84	leased
	ZS-SPC	South African Airways			11/1/86	
21140	VH-EBK	Qantas	238B	8/15/75	11/7/75	City of Wollongong
	VH-EBK	Air Pacific			1985	
21141	N40116	Wilmington Trust Co.	128	1/27/76	2/25/76	
	N40116	Air France			2/25/76	
	F-BPVQ	Air France			10/31/83	
21162	9V-SQE	Singapore	212B	3/19/76	3/30/76	
	N747BH	Boeing			7/11/83	
	N727PA	Pan American			6/26/84	
21174	YK-AHA	Syrianair	SP94	4/15/76	5/21/76	16 November
21175	YK-AHB	Syrianair	SP94	7/1/76	7/16/76	Arab Soladarity
21180	YI-AGN	Iraqi Airways	270C	5/27/76	6/24/76	Tigris
21181	YI-AGO	Iraqi Airways	270C	6/21/76	8/15/76	Euphrates
21182	VT-EDU	Air India	237B	12/15/75	12/23/75	Emperor Akbar
21189	N1791B	Boeing	287B	11/11/75		
	LV-LZD	Aerolineas Argentinas			12/16/76	leased
	N354AS	Boeing			1/14/82	
	G-VIRG	Virgin Air			1/14/84	leased
21190	4X-AXD	El Al	258C	10/22/75	12/31/75	
	4X-AXD	Cargo Airlines				leased
21213	G-BDPV	British Airways	136	2/25/76	4/8/76	
21217	EP-IAG	Iran Air	286B/CO	12/22/76	3/14/77	
21220	N1786B	Boeing	230B/SC	9/24/76		
	D-ABYJ	Lufthansa			11/24/76	Hessen
21221	D-ABYK	Lufthansa	230B/SC	12/4/76	12/15/76	Rheinland-Pfalz
21237	VH-EBL	Qantas	238B	6/14/76	7/1/76	
21238	N1790B	Boeing	236B	9/3/76		
	G-BDXA	British Airways			7/27/77	
21239	G-BDXB	British Airways	236B	2/22/77	6/17/77	
21240	G-BDXC	British Airways	236B	4/8/77	6/23/77	
21241	N8285V	Boeing	238B			
	G-BDXD	British Airways			4/78	

s/n	reg	carrier	series	ff	dd	remarks
21251	N1239E	Boeing	2D3B/CO	10/12/76		
	JY-AFA	Alia			4/13/77	
21252	JY-AFB	Alia	2D3B/CO	10/26/76	5/11/77	
	G-HUGE	BCAL			3/18/85	
	G-HUGE	British Airways			1986	*City of Exter*
21253	ZS-SPD	South African Airways	SP44	8/27/76	9/10/76	*Majuba*
	CN-RMS	Royal Air Maroc			3/14/85	
21254	ZS-SPE	South African Airways	SP44	11/5/76	11/22/76	*Hantam*
21255	N1783B	Boeing	228F	9/26/76		
	F-BPVR	Air France			10/13/76	
21263	ZS-SPF	South African Airways	SP44	1/14/77	1/31/77	*Soutpansberg*
21300	B-1862	Chinal Airlines	SP09	3/18/77	4/6/77	
21316	9V-SQF	Singapore Airlines	212B	6/19/77	6/27/77	
	N747BJ	Boeing			7/5/84	
	N724PA	Pan American			8/31/84	
21321	N619US	Northwest Orient	251F/SC	6/3/77	6/27/77	
21326	F-BPVS	Air France	228B/SC	3/4/77	4/4/77	
21350	G-BDXE	British Airways	2365B		3/78	
21351	G-BDXF	British Airways	236B		4/78	
21352	N8295V	Boeing	238B	7/11/77		
	VH-EBM	Qantas			8/15/77	
21353	VH-EBN	Qantas	238B	12/6/77	12/20/77	
21354	VH-ECA	Qantas	238B/CO	10/4/77	10/27/77	
21380	D-ABYL	Lufthansa	230B/SC		3/78	*Saarland*
21381	LN-RNA	SAS	283B/CO	8/24/77	10/27/77	
	LN-RNA	Scanair			4/82	leased
	LN-RNA	SAS			8/3/82	
	HK-2910	Avianca			8/3/82	leased w/o 11/27/83 Majorada del Campo, Spain
21429	F-BPVT	Air France	228B/SC	9/21/77	9/30/77	
21439	9V-SQG	Singapore Airlines	212B	8/31/77	9/14/77	
	N747BK	Boeing			12/12/84	
	N723PA	Pan American			1/16/85	
21441	N536PA	Pan American	SP21	4/77	5/6/77	*Clipper Lindberg*
	N145UA	United Airlines			2/11/86	
21446	VT-EFJ	Air India	237B		2/78	*Emperor Chandragupta*
21454	B-1864	China Airlines	209B/CO	4/78	4/78	
21468	N124BE	Air Gabon	2Q2B/SC	4/23/78	10/5/78	
	F-ODJG	Air Gabon			1978	
21473	VT-EFO	Air India	237B	6/19/78	6/30/78	*Emperor Kanishka* w/o 6/23/85 Atlantic Ocean off coast Ireland
21486	5-8113	IIAF	2J9F	11/28/77	12/22/77	
	5-8113	IAF			2/78	
	EP-NHN	Iran Air			1984	
21487	5-8114	IAF	2J9F	2/16/78	2/27/78	
	EP-ICA	Iran Air			11/80	
	5-8114	IAF			1/83	
	EP-NHQ	Iran Air			6/84	
21507	N8277V	Boeing	2J9F	9/18/78		
	5-8115	IAF			9/28/78	
	EP-ICB	Iran Air			9/80	
21514	N8293V	Boeing	2J9F	10/11/78		
	5-8116	IAF			10/23/78	
	EP-ICC	Iran Air			1980	w/o assumed

s/n	reg	carrier	series	ff	dd	remarks
21515	N1780B	Boeing	2B3F	8/21/78		
	F-GPAN	UTA			9/26/78	
	F-GPAN	National Airlines			3/1/84	leased
	F-GPAN	Saudia			3/1/84	leased
	F-GPAN	National Airlines			4/30/85	leased
	F-GPAN	UTA			4/30/85	
	F-GPAN	Air France			3/28/86	
21516	N1785B	Boeing	211B	9/15/78		
	C-GXRA	Wardair			6/9/78	
	G-GLYN	British Airways			1987	City of Perth
21517	C-GXRD	Wardair	211B	4/2/79	4/25/79	
	G-NIGB	British Airways			1987	City of Glouster
21536	G-BDXG	British Airways	236B	6/2/78	6/16/78	
21537	N1252E	Boeing	228B/SC	7/21/78		
	N1252E	Air France			8/7/78	
	F-BPVU	Air France				
21541	9K-ADA	Kuwait Airways	269B/CO	7/17/78	7/28/78	Al-Sabahiya
21542	9K-ADB	Kuwait Airways	269B/CO	8/3/78	8/17/78	Al-Jabaria
21543	9K-ADC	Kuwait Airways	269B/CO	2/14/79	2/28/79	Al-Mobarakiya
21547	N537PA	Pan American	SP21	5/5/78	6/9/78	Clipper Washington
	N146UA	United Airlines			2/11/86	
21548	N538PA	Pan American	SP21	6/30/78	7/12/78	Clipper Plymouth Rock
	N147UA	United Airlines			2/11/86	
21549	PH-BUK	KLM	206B/CO	8/17/78	9/1/78	Louis Bléroit
21550	PH-BUL	KLM	206B/CO	10/17/78	11/3/78	Charles A. Lindberg
	PH-BUL	KLM	206B/SU	6/18/85	converted	
21575	SF-DFZ	SAS	283B/CO	2/17/79	3/2/79	
	SF-DFZ	Nigeria Airways			6/3/83	leased
	LX-OCV	Luxair				leased
	EI-BWF	Guniss-Peat				
	EI-BWF	Philippine Airlines				leased
21576	F-BPVV	Air France	228F	7/27/78	8/9/78	
21588	D-ABYM	Lufthansa	230B/SC	10/3/78	10/20/78	Schleswig-Holstein
21589	N8291V	Boeing	230B	11/22/78		
	D-ABYN	Lufthansa			3/7/79	Baden-Württenburg
21590	D-AGYP	Lufthansa	230B	6/78	6/78	Niedersachsan
21591	D-ABYQ	Lufthansa	230B	12/1/78	12/31/78	Bremen
21592	D-ABYO	Lufthansa	230F	11/10/78	11/22/78	America
21594	4X-AXF	El Al	258C	6/7/78	6/16/78	
	4X-AXF	CAL Cargo Lines				leased
21604	N8286V	Boeing	SR81	11/3/78		
	JA8133	All Nippon Airways			12/21/78	
21605	JA8134	All Nippon Airways	SR81	12/9/78	12/20/78	
21606	JA8135	All Nippon Airways	SR81	2/21/79	2/28/79	
21614	5R-MFT	Air Madagascar	2B2B/CO	1/12/79	1/26/79	Tolom Piavotana
21615	CN-RME	Royal Air Maroc	2B6B/CO	9/6/78	6/29/78	
21627	C-GAGB	Air Canada	233B/CO	1/16/79	1/31/79	stored Toronto, 1983
21635	G-BDXH	British Airwyas	236B	3/14/79	3/27/79	
21643	D-ABYR	Lufthansa	230B/SC	12/16/78	1/11/79	Nordrhein Westfalen
	D-ABYR	Condor			1/11/79	leased
	D-ABYR	Lufthansa			5/2/80	
21644	D-ABYS	Lufthansa	230B/SC	1/23/79	2/8/79	Bayern
21648	N539PA	Pan American	SP21	3/30/79	4/30/79	Clipper Liberty Bell
	N148UA	United Airlines			2/11/86	
21649	N540PA	Pan American	SP21	5/1/79	5/11/79	Clipper Star of the Union

s/n	reg	carrier	series	ff	dd	remarks
	N149UA	United Airlines			2/11/86	
21650	LX-DCV	Cargolux	2R7F	1/23/79	1/31/79	
21652	HZ-HM1	Saudi Royal Flight	SP86	9/28/78	7/11/79	
	HZ-HM1B	Saudi Royal Flight			1984	registration change
21657	VH-EBO	Qantas	238B	9/8/78	9/18/78	*City of Elizabeth*
21658	VH-EBP	Qantas	238B	9/30/78	10/16/78	*City of Adelaide*
21659	PH-BUM	KLM	206B/CO	4/9/79	5/15/79	*Sir Charles E. Kingsford Smith*
	PH-BUM	KLM	206B/SU	12/1/85	converted	
21660	PH-BUN	KLM	206B/CO	4/3/79	4/17/79	*Anthony H. G. Fokker*
	PH-BUN	KLM	206B/SU		3/27/86	converted
21668	N1288E	Boeing	2J9F	9/17/79		
	N630US	Northwest Orient			9/15/83	
21678	JA8129	Japan Airlines	246B	2/24/79	3/6/79	
21679	JA8130	Japan Airlines	246B	5/31/79	6/14/79	
21680	JA8131	Japan Airlines	246B	6/20/79	6/28/79	
21681	JA8132	Japan Airlines	246B	6/27/79	7/27/79	
21682	N602BN	Braniff	227B	5/17/79	5/31/79	
	N602PE	People Express			5/83	leased
	N602PE	People Express				
	N635US	Northwest Oreint			2/28/85	
21683	9V-SQH	Singapore Airlines	212B	7/19/79	8/2/79	
	SX-OAC	Olympic Airlines			9/19/84	*Olympic Spirit*
21684	9V-SQI	Singapore Airlines	212B	8/9/79	8/16/79	
	SX-OAD	Olympic Airlines			4/1/85	*Olympic Flame*
21704	N622US	Northwest Orient	251B	2/15/79	9/24/79	
21705	N623US	Northwest Orient	251B	5/11/79	5/25/79	
21706	N624US	Northwest Orient	251B	5/26/79	6/6/79	
21707	N625US	Northwest Orient	251B	6/8/79	6/17/79	
21708	N626US	Northwest Orient	251B	6/21/79	6/28/79	
21709	N627US	Northwest Orient	251B	12/21/79	1/2/80	
21725	N1789B	Boeing	287B	12/8/79		
	LV-MLO	Aerolineas Argentinas			1/13/79	
	LV-MLO	Flying Tigers			7/4/83	leased
21726	LV-MLP	Aerolineas Argentinas	287B	10/1/79	10/11/79	
21727	LV-MLR	Aerolineas Argentinas	287B	10/5/79	10/26/79	
21730	HK-2300	Avianca	259B/CO	5/11/79	6/8/79	
	HK-2300	Chemco Leasing			5/30/83	
	HK-2980	Avianca			5/30/83	leased
21731	N1252E	Air France	228B/SC		3/29/79	
	F-BPVX	Air France				
21737	4X-AXG	El Al	258F	3/7/79	3/19/79	
	4X-AXG	Cargo Air Lines				leased
21743	N904PA	Pan American	221F	7/5/79	7/25/79	
	JA8165	Japan Airlines			12/20/83	
21744	N905PA	Pan American	221F	8/11/79	8/28/79	
	JA8160	Japan Airlines			10/82	
21745	F-BPVY	Air France	228B	4/13/79	4/28/79	
21746	VR-HKG	Cathay Pacific	267B	7/4/79	7/20/79	
21758	EP-IAD	Iran Air	SP86	4/26/79	7/12/79	
21759	EP-IAM	Iran Air	186B	6/20/79	8/2/79	
21760	EP-IAN	Iran Air	186B			NTU
21761	EP-IAP	Iran Air	186B			NTU
21762	EP-IAR	Iran Air	186B			NTU
21764	N703SW	Seaboard World	245F	8/25/79	9/6/79	
	N813FT	Flying Tigers			10/1/80	

s/n	reg	carrier	series	ff	dd	remarks
21772	HL7443	Korean Air Lines	2B5B	3/8/79	3/23/79	
21773	HL7445	Korean Air LInes	2B5B	3/23/79	4/11/79	w/o 11/18/80 Seoul
21782	HS-TGA	Thai International	2D7B	10/1/79	11/2/79	*Visuthakastriyka*
21783	HS-TGB	Thai International	2D7B	12/3/79	12/15/79	*Sirisobhakya*
21784	HS-TGC	Thai International	2D7B	12/3/79	12/15/79	*Dararasmi*
21785	N603BN	Braniff	SP27	10/7/79	10/30/79	
	N351AS	Boeing			1/23/81	stored Boeing
	A40-SO	Government of Oman			2/7/85	
21786	N604BN	Braniff	SP27	11/29/79	4/23/80	
	LV-OHV	Aerolineas Argentinas			9/12/80	
21787	F-BPVZ	Air France	228F	9/7/79	9/18/79	
21825	AP-BAK	Pakistan International	240B/CO	7/2/79	7/26/79	
21827	N806FT	Flying Tiger Line	249F	10/15/79	10/31/79	*Robert W. Prescott*
21828	N807FT	Flying Tiger Line	249F	11/1/79	12/11/79	w/o
21829	VT-EFU	Air India	237B	8/3/79	8/14/79	*Krishna Deva Raya*
21830	G-BDXI	British Airways	236B	2/16/80	3/5/80	
21831	G-BDXJ	British Airways	236B	3/26/80	5/2/80	
21832	N1288E	Boeing	2F6B	12/14/79		
	N741PR	Philippine Airlines			12/21/79	
21833	N1289E	Boeing	2F6B	1/7/80		
	N742PR	Philippine Airlines			2/22/80	
21834	N1290E	Boeing	2F6B	1/17/80		
	N743PR	Philippine Airlines			3/21/80	
21835	F-GBOX	UTA	2B3F	7/25/79	8/6/79	
	F-GBOX	Saudia			1985	leased
	F-GBOX	UTA			1985	leased
21841	N704SW	Seaboard World	245F	9/16/79	9/29/79	
	N814FT	Flying Tiger Line			10/1/80	
21843	B-1866	China Airlines	209B	7/16/79	7/31/79	
21848	PH-BUO	KLM	206B	9/6/79	9/22/79	*The Missouri*
	PH-BUO	KLM	206B/SU	1/29/85	converted	
21922	JA8136	All Nippon Airways	SR81	8/21/79	9/10/79	
21923	JA8137	All Nippon Airways	SR81	8/25/79	9/10/79	
21924	JA8138	All Nippon Airways	SR81	12/18/79	1/16/80	
21925	JA8139	All Nippon Airways	SR81	1/15/80	2/15/80	
21932	B-2442	CAAC	SPJ6	2/14/80	2/29/80	
21933	B-2444	CAAC	SPJ6	6/6/801	6/26/80	
21934	B-2446	CAAC	SPJ6			NTU
21935	9V-SQJ	Singapore Airlines	212B	9/17/79	9/25/79	
	SX-OAE	Olympic Airways			12/25/85	*Olympic Peace*
21936	9V-SQK	Singapore Airlines	212B	9/25/79	10/1/79	
	VT-ENQ	Air India			1987	*The Himalaya*
21937	9V-SQL	Singapore Airlines	212B	1/14/80	2/1/80	
	9V-SQL	Int'l Lease Finance			3/89	
	G-VRGN	Virgin Air			7/89	
21938	9V-SQM	Singapore Airlines	212B	3/10/80	4/10/80	
21939	9V-SQN	Singapore Airlines	212B		5/80	
	9V-SQN	Int's Lease Finance			3/89	
	G-TKYO	Virgin Air			4/89	
21940	9V-SQO	Singapore Airlines	212B	6/12/80	6/27/80	
21941	9V-SQP	Singapore Airlines	212B	8/15/80	9/12/80	
21942	9V-SQQ	Singapore Airlines	212B	9/11/80	9/25/80	
21943	9V-SQR	Singapore Airlines	212B	10/16/80	10/30/80	
21944	9V-SQS	Singapore Airlines	212B	2/18/81	3/19/81	
21961	N58201	Trans World Airlines	SP31	12/2/79	4/14/79	
	A6-SMR	United Arab Emirates Gvt		3/1/85		

s/n	reg	carrier	series	ff	dd	remarks
21962	N57202	Trans World Airlines	SP31	3/12/80	3/21/80	
	N57202	Jet Aviation			4/4/84	
	N57202	Jet Associates			12/85	
	N57202	American Airlines			10/86	
21963	N57203	Trans World Airlines	SP31	4/11/80	5/8/80	
	N57203	American Airlines			10/86	
21964	N741TV	Transamerica Airlines	271C	11/30/79	12/21/79	
	N741TV	UTA			5/3/85	leased
	N741TV	Transamerica Airlines			5/16/86	
21965	N742TV	Transamerica Airlines	271C	3/8/80	3/26/80	
21966	VR-HIA	Cathay Pacific	267B	4/7/80	4/24/80	
21977	VH-ECB	Qantas	238B/CO	10/25/79	11/14/79	*City of Swan Hill*
21982	F-GCBA	Air France	228B	1/30/80	2/29/80	
21991	N605BN	Braniff	227B	3/25/80		NTU
	N8284V	Boeing				ordered by Air Algerie
	N633US	Northwest Orient			4/19/84	
21992	N606BN	Braniff	SP27	5/19/80	5/30/80	
	N529PA	Pam American			9/23/83	
	N150UA	United Airlines			2/11/86	
21993	VT-EGA	Air India	237B	12/11/79	12/21/79	*Samudra Gupta*
21994	VT-EGB	Air India	237B	2/7/80	2/20/80	*Mahendra Varman*
21995	VT-EGC	Air India	237B	2/28/80	4/4/80	*Harsha Vardhana*
22063	JA8144	Japan Airlines	246F	2/24/80	3/17/80	
22064	JA8140	Japan Airlines	246B		11/79	
22065	JA8141	Japan Airlines	246B	11/12/79	12/3/79	
22066	JA8142	Japan Airlines	246B	1/21/80	1/31/80	
22067	JA8143	Japan Airlines	246B	1/25/80	2/14/80	
22077	AP-BAT	PIA	240B/CO	2/2/80	3/7/80	
22105	5A-DIJ	Libyan Arab Airlines	2L5B	2/28/81		NTU
	PP-VNA	Boeing			1/30/81	
	PP-VNA	Orient Leasing			1/30/81	
	PP-VNA	Varig			1/30/81	leased
22106	5A-DIK	Libyan Arab Airlines	2L5B	3/26/80		NTU
	PP-VNB	Beoing			2/9/81	
	PP-VNB	Orient Leasing			2/9/81	
	PP-VNB	Varig			2/9/81	leased
22107	5A-DIL	Libyan Arab Airlines	2L5B			NTU
	N1290E	Boeing				
	PP-VNC	Orient Leasing			3/5/81	
	PP-VNC	Varig		12/5/80	3/5/81	
22145	VH-EBQ	Qantas	238B	11/28/79	12/11/79	*City of Branbury*
22149	VR-HIB	Cathay Pacific	267B	6/30/80	7/16/80	
22150	N705SW	Seaboard World	245F	9/22/80		NTU
	N815FT	Flying Tigers			10/3/80	*W. Henry Renninger*
22151	N706SW	Seaboard World	245F	10/3/80		NTU
	N816FT	Flying Tigers		10/14/80		*Henry H. Heguy*
22169	TU-TAP	Air Afrique	254F	9/12/80	10/3/80	
	TU-TAP	National Airlines			3/1/84	leased
	TU-TAP	Saudia			3/1/84	leased
	TU-TAP	National Airlines			4/1/85	leased
	TU-TAP	Air Afrique			4/1/85	
	TU-TAP	Cargolux			5/85	leased
	TU-TAP	Air Afrique			9/24/85	
	TU-TAP	Japan Leasing Corp.			9/24/85	
	TU-TAP	Korean Air			9/24/85	leased
	LX-TAP	Cargolux			9/24/85	leased

s/n	reg	carrier	series	ff	dd	remarks
	HL7474	Korean Air			4/11/86	leased
22170	ZS-SAA	South African Airways	244B/CO	10/24/80		NTU
	ZS-SAR	South African Airways			11/6/80	Waterberg
22171	ZS-SAB	South African Airways	244B/CO	11/12/80		
	ZS-SAS	South African Airways			11/24/80	
22234	N607BN	Braniff	227B	1/14/81		NTU
	N1607B	Braniff				
	N8285V	Air Algerie				NTU
	N634US	Boeing			5/29/84	
22235	N609BN	Braniff	227B			NTU
22236	N612BN	Braniff	227B			NTU
22237	N809FT	Flying Tiger Line	249F	7/31/80		NTU
	N810FT	Flying Tiger Line			9/12/80	
	N810FT	Cargo Air Lines			1980	leased
	N810FT	Flying Tiger Line			1980	Clifforn G. Groh
22238	EC-DIA	Iberia	256B	4/23/80	5/1/80	Tiriso de Molina
22239	EC-DIB	Iberia	256B	5/2/80	5/27/80	Cervantes
22245	N808FT	Flying Tiger Line	249F	6/20/80	7/3/80	William E. Bartling
22246	PK-GSA	Garuda	2U3B	6/12/80	7/2/80	
22247	PK-GSB	Garuda	2U3B	7/3/80	7/30/80	
22248	PK-GSC	Garuda	2U3B	8/8/80	8/26/80	
22254	4X-AXH	El Al	258B	12/6/79	12/21/79	
22272	N1289E	Air France	228B/SC	6/18/80	7/3/80	
22291	JA8145	All Nippon Airways	SR81	5/3/80	5/16/80	
22292	JA8146	All Nirways	SR81	5/23/80	6/16/80	
22293	JA8147	All Nippon Airways	SR81	8/15/80	11/25/80	
22294	JA8148	All Nippon Airways	SR81	9/30/80	11/25/80	
22297	LV-OEP	Aerolineas Argentinas	287B	11/4/80	11/18/80	
22298	B-1861	China Airlines	SP09	4/18/80		NTU
	B-1880	China Airlines			4/30/80	
22299	B-1885	China Airlines	209F	7/11/80		NTU
	B1894	China Airlines			7/24/80	
22303	G-BDXK	British Airways	236B	3/30/83		
22302	N608BN	Braniff	SP27	12/2/80		NTU
	N1608B	Braniff				stored Seattle
	N1301E	CAAC			6/11/83	
22304	G-BDXM	British Airways	236B	1/24/81		NTU
	9M-MHI	Malaysian Airlines System		3/14/82		
22305	N8280V	Boeing	236B	2/12/81		
	G-BDXL	British Airways			3/14/82	
	G-BDXL	British Airtours			2/10/84	
	G-BDXL	British Airways			10/31/84	
22306	G-BDXK	British Airways	236F	9/19/80		NTU
	G-KILO	British Airways			9/30/80	
	VR-HVY	Cathay Pacific			3/15/82	
22337	HS-TGF	Thai International	2D7B	9/11/80	9/24/80	Phimara
22363	D-ABYT	Lufthansa	230B/SC	11/4/80	11/19/80	Hamburg
22366	YI-AGP	Iraqi Airways	270C	6/25/82	7/15/82	Shat-al-Arab
22376	N1295E	KLM	206B	8/6/80	9/11/80	The Ganges
	N1295E	KLM	206B/SU		12/13/84	converted
22378	TJ-CAB	Cameroon Airlines	2H7B/CO	2/6/81	2/26/81	
22379	N1298E	KLM	206B	11/6/80	12/15/80	The Indus
	N1298E	KLM	206B/SU		3/11/85	converted
22380	N1301E	KLM	206B/CO	8/21/81		NTU
	N1309E	KLM			9/29/81	ADM Richard E. Byrd
	N1309E	KLM	206B/SU		1/86	converted

s/n	reg	carrier	series	ff	dd	remarks
22381	OY-KHB	SAS	283B/CO	12/20/80		
	N4501Q	SAS			2/17/81	
	EI-BTS	GPA			1988	
	EI-BTS	Philippine Airlines			1988	leased
22382	N744PR	Philippine Airlines	2F6B	12/2/80	12/12/80	
22388	N629US	Northwest Orient	251F	4/1/80	4/18/80	
22389	N628US	Northwest Orient	251B	3/21/80	4/8/80	
22390	LX-ECV	Cargolux	2R7F	9/30/80	10/10/80	
	B-198	China Airlines			2/26/85	
	B-198	Cargolux			2/26/85	leased
	B-198	China Airlines			6/2/85	
22403	N743TV	Transamerica Airlines	271C	5/1/81	6/1/81	
	N743TV	Saudia			4/14/85	leased
	N743TV	Transamerica Airlines			4/1/86	
	N743TV	Cargolux			4/1/86	leased
22404	N744TV	Transamerica Airlines	271C			NTU
22405	N745TV	Transamerica Airlines	271C			NTU
22427	F-GCBC	Air France	228B/SC	10/7/80	10/21/80	w/o 12/2/85, Rio de Janerio, Brazil
22428	F-GDBD	Air France	228B/SC	12/23/80		NTU
	N130SE	Air France			3/2/81	
	F-GCBD	Air France			6/81	
22429	VR-HIC	Cathay Pacific	267B	12/5/80	12/19/80	
22442	G-BDXN	British Airways	236B		4/8/82	
	9M-MHJ	Malaysian Airline System		4/8/82		
22446	B-1886	China Airlines	209B	4/7/81	4/17/81	
22447	B-1888	China Airlines	209B	2/17/82	3/4/82	
22454	EC-DLC	Iberia	256B	2/6/81	2/18/81	
	EC-DLC	Iberia	256B/CO		10/4/84	converted
22455	EC-DLD	Iberia	256B	3/12/81	3/24/81	
	EC-DLD	Iberia	256B/CO		11/29/84	converted
22471	HS-TGG	Thai International	2D7B	1/16/81	3/16/81	*Sriwanha*
22472	HS-TGD	Thai International				NTU
	N6066U	Boeing		5/16/84		
	HS-TGS	Thai International			6/1/84	*Chainarai*
22477	JA8151	Japan Airlines	246F	11/26/80	4/15/81	
22478	JA8149	Japan Airlines	246B	11/26/80	3/13/81	
22479	N1783B	Boeing	246B	12/13/80		
	JA8150	Japan Airlines	246B		3/19/81	
22480	HL7451	Korean Air Lines	2B5F	4/30/80	6/25/80	
	HL7451	Saudia			5/27/86	leased
22481	N5573F	Boeing	2B5F	6/4/80		
	HL7452	Korean Air Lines			6/25/80	
	HL7452	Saudia			2/27/81	leased
	HL7452	Korean Air Lines			5/11/81	
	HL7452	Korean Air Lines			2/17/83	leased
	HL7452	Korean Air Lines			2/13/84	leased
22482	HL7454	Korean Air Lines	2B5B	10/17/80	11/13/80	
22483	HL7456	Korean Air Lines	SPB5	12/22/80	1/22/81	
22484	HL7457	Korean Air Lines	SPB5	1/30/81	3/18/81	
22485	HL7458	Korean Air Lines	2B5B	3/6/81	4/13/81	
22486	N8281V	Boeing	2B5F	4/10/81		
	HL7459	Korean Air Lines			5/8/81	
	HL7459	Saudia			5/8/81	leased
	HL7459	Korean Air Lines			2/28/84	
22487	N6069D	Boeing	3B5			

s/n	reg	carrier	series	ff	dd	remarks
	HL7468	Korean Air Lines			12/12/84	
22489	N6009F	Boeing	3B5	3/30/85		
	HL7469	Korean Air Lines			4/15/85	
22495	VH-EAA	Qantas	SP38	1/11/81	1/19/81	*City of Gold Coast/ Tweed*
22496	LN-RNB	SAS	283B/CO	8/26/81		NTU
	N4502R	SAS			10/22/81	
	N4502R	Nigeria Airways			6/3/83	leased
	N4502R	SAS			1983	
	N4502R	GPA			2/17/89	
	EI-BZA	SAS			2/17/89	leased
22498	N8281V	Boeing	168B	3/2/81		
	HZ-AIA	Saudia			4/24/81	
22499	HZ-AIB	Saudia	168B	3/23/81	4/2/81	
22500	HZ-AIC	Saudia	168B	4/23/81	5/20/81	
22501	HZ-AID	Saudia	168B	5/8/81	5/21/81	
22502	HZ-AIE	Saudia	168B		7/81	
22503	HZ-AIF	Saudia	SP68		6/81	
22506	I-DEMC	Alitalia	243B/CO	11/14/80	11/26/80	*Taormina*
22507	I-DEMD	Alitalia	243B/CO	11/26/80	12/12/80	*Cortina d'Ampezzo*
22508	I-DEMF	Alitalia	243B/CO	12/11/80	12/22/80	*Portofino*
22510	I-DEMG	Alitalia	243B		8/81	*Cervinia*
22511	I-DEML	Alitalia	243B		9/81	*Sorrento*
22512	I-DEMN	Alitalia	243B	9/21/81	11/5/81	*Portocervo*
22513	I-DEMP	Alitalia	243B	11/2/81	12/3/81	*Capri*
22514	F-BTDG	UTA	2B3B/CO	4/1/81	4/23/81	
	F-BTDG	UTA	2B3B/SU		3/86	converted
22515	F-BTDH	UTA	2B3B/CO	4/17/81	5/5/81	
	F-BTDH	UTA	2B3B/SU		5/15/86	converted
22530	VR-HID	Cathay Pacific	267B		6/81	*St. Resa*
22545	I-DEMR	Alitalia	243F	10/15/81	12/18/81	
22547	B-1882	China Airlines	SP09			NTU
	N4508H	Wilmington Trust		7/20/81	9/30/81	
	N4508H	China Airlines			9/30/81	leased
22579	JY-AFS	Alia	2D3B	3/9/81	3/26/81	
	G-CITB	British Airways			1986	*City of Norwick*
22592	LV-OOZ	Aerolineas Argentinas	2B7B		8/81	
22593	LV-OPA	Aerolines Argentinas	2B7B	12/16/81	1/23/82	
22594	JA8152	All Nippon Airways	SR81	2/18/81	2/27/81	
22595	JA8153	All Nippon Airways	SR81	3/29/81	5/28/81	
22614	N8296V	Boeing	238B	6/24/80		
	VH-EBR	Qantas			9/30/80	leased *City of Hobart*
22615	VH-ECC	Qantas	238B/CO	9/29/80	10/15/80	*City of Shepparton*
22616	N6500C	Boeing	238B	9/25/81		
	VH-EBS	Qantas			11/30/81	*City of Longreach*
22617	VH-EBT	Qantas	238B			NTU
22668	D-ABYU	Lufthansa	230F		9/81	*Asia*
22669	D-ABYW	Lufthansa	230B/SC	11/19/81	12/23/81	*Berlin*
22670	D-ABYX	Lufthansa	230B	12/1/81	2/25/83	*Köln*
22671	D-ABYY	Lufthansa	230B	12/4/82	12/20/82	*Münchin*
22672	VH-EAB	Qantas	SP38		8/81	*Winton*
22678	N4508E	Air France	228F		9/11/81	
22704	B6005C	Boeing	357	10/5/87		
	N8277V	Boeing				
	HB-IGC	Swissair			3/19/83	*Bern*

s/n	reg	carrier	series	ff	dd	remarks
22705	N1784B	Boeing	357/SCD	2/14/83		
	HB-IGD	Swissair			3/5/83	*Basel*
22709	JA8156	All Nippon Airways	SR81	9/21/81	12/17/81	
22710	JA8157	All Nippon Airways	SR81	10/15/81	12/17/81	
22711	JA8158	All Nippon Airways	SR81	4/1/82	6/17/82	
22712	JA8159	All Nippon Airways	SR81	10/23/82	11/12/82	
22722	ZK-NZV	Air New Zeland	219B	5/6/81	5/22/81	*Astea*
22723	ZK-NZW	Air New Zeland	219B	5/22/81	6/9/81	*Tainui*
22724	ZK-NZX	Air New Zeland	219B		6/81	*Takitimu*
22725	ZK-NZY	Boeing	219B	5/27/82		
	ZK-NZY	Air New Zeland			6/22/82	*Te Araw*
22740	9K-ADD	Kuwait Airways	269B/CO	1/14/82	1/20/82	*Al-Salmiya*
22745	JA8154	Japan Airlines	246B	11/4/81	11/17/81	
22746	JA8155	Japan Airlines	246B	11/17/81	12/15/81	
22747	HZ-AIG	Saudia	168B	12/11/81	1/82	
22748	HZ-AIH	Saudia	168B	2/3/82	3/17/82	
22749	HZ-AII	Saudia	168B	3/19/82	4/2/82	
22750	N6046P	Boeing	SP68			
	HZ-AIJ	Saudia			5/82	
22764	N8296V	Boeing	256B	1/25/82		
	EC-DNP	Iberia			2/26/82	
22768	PK-GSE	Garuda	23B	4/24/82	5/5/82	
22769	PK-GSF	Garuda	2U3B	5/8/82	5/18/82	
22791	N6018N	Boeing	219B	8/5/82		
	ZK-NZZ	Air New Zeland			8/25/82	*Tokomaru*
22794	N4506H	Air France	228B/SC	3/17/82	3/26/82	
22805	N4522V	Wilmington Trust	SP09	6/10/82	6/10/82	
	N4522V	China Airlines			6/10/82	leased
22858	YI-ALM	Iraqi Government	SP70	8/2/82	8/30/82	
22870	F-GDUT	UTA	3B3			NTU
	N6067B	Boeing		12/10/82		
	N8278V	Boeing				
	F-GDUA	UTA			3/1/83	w/o 3/16/85 Paris CDG 22871
	F-GDUB	UTA	3B3			NTU
22872	VR-HIE	Cathay Pacific	267B	7/9/82	7/23/82	
22939	N5454F	Boeing	228B	8/25/82		
	F-GCBG	Air France			10/1/82	
22969	N8289V	Boeing	243B	2/11/83		
	I-DEMS	Alitalia			2/28/83	*Monte Argentario*
22970	N8279V	Boeing	344	2/16/83		
	ZS-SAT	South African Airways			5/2/83	*Johannesburg*
22971	N8296V	Boeing	344	3/27/83		
	ZS-SAU	South African Airways			4/14/83	*Cape Town/Kaapstad*
22989	N211JL	Japan Airlines	246B	10/7/82	12/14/82	
22990	N6046B	Boeing	246B	4/25/83		
	JA8161	Japan Airlines			6/16/83	
22991	N5573K	Boeing	246B	5/17/83		
	JA8162	Japan Airlines			6/6/83	
22995	HB-IGE	Swissair	357	9/22/83		
	N221GE	Swissair			12/16/83	*Genéve*
22996	HB-IGF	Swissair	357			NTU
	N221GF	Swissair		9/12/83	11/30/83	*Zürich*
22997	HB-IGG	Swissair	357		1/89	*Ticino*
23026	N6006C	Boeing	312	4/15/83		
	N8279CV	Boeing			4/83	
	9V-SKA	Singapore Airlines			4/20/83	

s/n	reg	carrier	series	ff	dd	remarks
23027	9V-SKB	Singapore Airlines	312	6/12/83		
	N116KB	Singapore Airlines			6/21/83	
23028	9V-SKC	Singapore Airlines	312	6/23/83		
	N117KC	Singapore Airlines			6/30/83	
23029	9V-SKD	Singapore Airlines	312	11/11/83		
	N118KD	Singapore Airlines			11/22/83	
23030	9V-SKE	Singapore Airlines	312	2/1/84		
	N119KE	Singapore Airlines			2/24/84	
23031	9V-SKF	Singapore Airlines	312	2/18/84		
	N120KF	Singapore Airlines			2/28/84	
23032	9V-SKG	Singapore Airlines	312	10/17/84		
	N121KG	Singapore Airlines			10/30/84	
23033	9V-SKH	Singapore Airlines	312	3/1/85		
	N122KH	Singapore Airlines			3/20/85	
23048	N6066U	Boeing	267B	5/13/83		
	VR-HIF	Cathay Pacific			5/22/83	
23056	N4548M	Int'l Lease Finance	306/CO	9/15/83	9/30/83	
	N4548M	KLM			9/30/83	*Sir Frank Whittle*
23067	JA8163	Japan Airlines	346	10/10/83		
	N212JL	Japan Airlines			11/29/83	
23068	JA8164	Japan Airlines	346	10/26/83		
	N213JL	Japan Airlines			12/8/83	
23070	N1784B	Boeing	3G1	12/15/83		
	HZ-HM1A	Saudi Royal Flight			12/22/83	
23071	N1781B	Boeing	2J6B/CO	12/6/83		
	B-2446	CAAC			12/20/83	
23111	N631US	Northwest Orient	251B	2/28/84	4/2/84	
23112	N632US	Northwest Orient	251B	3/27/84	5/1/84	
23120	N5573B	Boeing	267B	4/17/84		
	VR-HIH	Cathay Pacific			4/27/84	
23137	N4551N	Int'l Lease Finance	306/CO	4/9/84	9/13/84	
	N4551N	KLM			9/13/84	*Sir Geoffery de Havilland*
23138	N6066Z	Boeing	281F			
	JA8167	All Nippon Airways			12/13/84	
	JA8167	Nippon Air Cargo			12/13/84	leased
23139	N6046P	Boeing	281F	2/20/85		
	JA8168	All Nippon Airways			2/28/85	
	JA8168	Nippon Air Cargo			2/28/85	leased
23149	N5573B	Boeing	346			
	JA8163	Japan Airlines			12/6/84	
23150	N1781B	Boeing	346B			
	JA8164	Japan Airlines			12/4/84	
23151	N1786B	Boeing	346	1/17/85		
	JA8166	Japan Airlines			2/4/85	
23221	N6018N	Boeing	367	5/31/85		
	VR-HII	Cathay Pacific			6/13/85	
23222	N1784B	Boeing	338	10/6/84		
	VH-EBT	Qantas			11/13/84	*City of Canberra*
23223	N5573P	Boeing	338	12/21/84		
	VH-EBU	Qantas			1/24/85	*City of Sidney*
23224	N6005C	Boeing	338	3/21/85		
	VH-EBV	Qantas			4/15/85	*City of Melborne*
23243	N123KJ	Singapore Airlines	312	4/19/85	4/30/85	
23244	N124KK	Singapore Airlines	312	4/23/85	9/24/85	
23245	N125KL	Singapore Airlines	312	11/5/85	12/11/85	

s/n	reg	carrier	series	ff	dd	remarks
23246	9V-SKP	Singapore Airlines	312			NTU
23262	N6005C	Boeing	368	6/13/85		
	HZ-AIK	Saudia			7/12/85	
23263	N6009F	Boeing	368	7/26/85		
	HZ-AIL	Saudia			6/2/85	
23264	N6046P	Boeing	368	9/9/85		
	HZ-AIM	Saudia			8/21/85	
23265	N6046P	Boeing	368	10/11/85		
	HZ-AIN	Saudia			12/20/85	
23266	N6005C	Boeing	368	10/9/85		
	HZ-AIO	Saudia			10/24/85	
23267	N6055X	Boeing	368	1/3/86		
	HZ-AIP	Saudia			1/17/86	
23268	N6005C	Boeing	368	1/14/86		
	HZ-AIQ	Saudia			3/14/86	
23269	N6038E	Boeing	368	5/1/85		
	HZ-AIR	Saudia			7/24/86	
23270	N6046P	Boeing	368	8/86		
	HZ-AIS	Saudia			9/86	
23271	N6038N	Boeing	368	10/86		
	HZ-AIT	Saudia			11/86	
23286	N6055X	Boeing	230B	5/16/85		
	D-ABYZ	Lufthansa			5/24/85	*Frankfort*
23287	N603BE	Boeing	230B	6/21/85		
	D-ABZA	Lufthansa			6/28/85	*Düseldorf*
23300	N6009F	Boeing	243B	5/8/85		
	I-DEMT	Alitalia			5/29/85	*Montecatini*
23301	N6018N	Boeing	243B/SC	7/12/85		
	I-DEMV	Alitalia			7/24/85	*Sestriere*
	I-DEMV	Egyptair			7/3/86	leased
23348	N6005F	Boeing	230F	10/1/85		
	D-ABZB	Lufthansa			10/15/85	*Europa*
23389	N601BN	Boeing	246B	3/1/86		
	JA8169	Japan Airlines			3/16/89	
23390	N6009F	Boeing	SR46/SU	2/26/86		
	JA8170	Japan Airlines			3/24/86	
23391	JA8171	Japan Airlines	246F			
23392	N6005C	Boeing	367	2/8/86		
	VR-HIJ	Cathay Pacific			2/14/86	
23393	N6046P	Boeing	230B	1/24/86		
	D-ABZC	Lufthansa			2/14/86	*Hannover*
23394	N6005C	Boeing	341	11/22/85		
	PP-VNH	Varig			12/10/85	
23395	N6009F	Boeing	341	12/13/85		
	PP-VNI	Varig			12/19/85	
23407	N6005C	Boeing	230B	3/31/86		
	D-ABZD	Lufthansa			4/10/86	*Kiel*
23408	N6055X	Boeing	338	3/19/86		
	VH-EBW	Qantas			3/31/86	*City of Brisbane*
23409	N6065Y	Boeing	312/CO	3/10/86		
	9V-SKM	Singapore Airlines			3/25/86	
23410	9V-SKN	Singapore Airlines	312/CO		3/87	
23413	F-GDUE	UTA	383/SC	1/23/86		
	F-GETA	UTA			1/31/86	
23439	N6005C	Boeing	329/CO	5/29/86		
	OO-SGC	Sabena			6/10/86	

s/n	reg	carrier	series	ff	dd	remarks
23461	N6066B	Boeing	2J6B	11/30/85		
	B-2448	CAAC			12/10/85	
23476	I-DEMW	Alitalia	243/SCD	6/6/86	6/13/86	*Spoledo*
23480	N6018N	Boeing	3B3	4/14/86		
	F-GETB	UTA			4/24/86	
23482	N6009F	Boeing	346	4/6/86		
	JA8173	Japan Airlines			4/15/86	
23501	N6055X	Boeing	281B	6/16/86		
	JA8174	All Nippon Airways			6/25/86	
23502	N60659	Boeing	281B	6/23/86		
	JA8175	All Nippon Airways			7/2/86	
23508	N6055X	Boeing	306/SCD	1986		
	PH-BUX	KLM			1986	*Leonardo di Vinci*
23509	N6038E	Boeing	230F	4/86		
	D-ABZE	Lufthansa			5/1/86	*Stuttgart*
23611	N6046P	Boeing	228B	5/86		
	F-GCBH	Air France			5/86	
23621	N6046P	Boeing	230F	6/86		
	D-ABZF	Lufthansa			7/86	*Australia*
23622	N6046P	Boeing	230F	6/86		
	D-ABZH	Lufthansa			8/86	*Bonn*
23676	N6009F	Boeing	228B			
	F-GCBI	Air France			1986	
23652	PH-MCE	Virgin Atlantic	21AC		2/18/89	
23688	N6005C	Boeing	338	1986		
	VH-EBX	Qantas			1986	*City of Perth*
23719	N661US	Northwest Airlines	451		1988	
23720	N662US	Northwest Airlines	451		1989	
23721	N6046T	Boeing	3D7	1987		
	HS-TGD	Korean Airlines			1988	*Suchada*
23722	N60668	Boeing	3D7	1987		
	HS-TGE	Korean Airlines			1988	*Chutamat*
23736	N151UA	United Airlines	222B		1987	
23737	N152UA	United Airlines	222B		1987	
23746	B-2450	China Airlines	2J6B	7/87	7/87	
23818	N663US	Northwest Airlines	451		1989	
23819	N664US	Northwest Airlines	451		1989	
23820	N665US	Northwest Airlines	451		1989	
23821	N666Us	Northwest Airlines	451		1989	
23999	PH-BFA	KLM	406		1989	*City of Atlanta*
24000	PH-BFB	KLM	406		1989	*City of Bangkok*
24061	N5573V	Boeing	412	3/15/89		
	9V-SMA	Singapore Airlines			3/29/90	
24062	N6500C	Boeing	412	2/6/89		
	9V-SMB	Singapore Airlines			3/18/89	
24067	N6018N	Boeing	228B			
	F-GCBJ	Air France			1988	
24138	N6005C	Boeing	230F			
	D-ABZI	Lufthansa			7/88	*Australia*
24158	N6055X	Boeing	228F			
	F-GCBK	Air France			1988	
24322	N171UA	United Airlines	422	4/89	5/89	
24354	VH-OJA	Qantas	438		1989	*City of Canberra*
24363	N172UA	United Airlines	422	5/89	6/89	
24380	N173UA	United Airlines	422	7/89	8/79	
24381	N174UA	United Airlines	422	7/89	8/89	

HL7410	20770	HZ-AIS	23270	JA1831	21680	LN-AET	20120	N133TW	19957
HL7411	20771	HZ-AIT	23271	JA8132	21681	LN-RNA	21381	N134TW	19958
HL7440	20372	HZ-HM1	21652	JA8133	21604	LN-RNB	22496	N1352B	20235
HL7441	20373	HZ-HM1A	23070	JA8134	21605			N140UA	21022
HL7442	20559	HZ-HM1B	21652	JA8135	21606	**LV Aregentina**		N141UA	21023
HL7443	21772			JA8136	21922			N142UA	21024
HL7445	21773	**I Italy**		JA8137	21923	LV-OHV	21786	N143UA	21025
HL7447	20493			JA8138	21924	LV-LRG	19896	N144UA	21026
HL7447	20493	I-DEMA	19729	JA8139	21925	LV-LZD	21189	N145UA	21025
HL7451	22480	I-DEMB	20520	JA8140	22064	LV-MLO	21725	N145UA	21441
HL7452	22481	I-DEMC	22506	JA8141	22065	LV-MLP	21726	N146UA	21547
HL7454	22482	I-DEMD	22507	JA8142	22066	LV-MLR	21727	N147UA	21548
HL7456	22483	I-DEME	19730	JA8143	22067	LV-OEP	22297	N148UA	21648
HL7457	22484	I-DEMF	22508	JA8144	22063	LV-OOZ	22592	N149UA	21649
HL7458	22485	I-DEMG	22510	JA8145	22291	LV-OPA	22593	N14936	20105
HL7459	22486	I-DEML	22511	JA8146	22292			N14937	20106
HL7463	20770	I-DEMN	22512	JA1847	22293	**LX Luxebbourg**		N14939	20108
HL7464	20771	I-DEMO	19731	JA8148	22294			N14943	20102
HL7468	22487	I-DEMP	22513	JA8149	22478	LX-DCV	21650	N150UA	21992
HL7469	22489	I-DEMR	22545	JA8150	22479	LX-ECV	22390	N151UA	23736
HL7471	20652	I-DEMS	22969	JA8151	22477	LX-LTM	21132	N152UA	23737
HL7474	22169	I-DEMT	23300	JA8152	22594	LX-MCV	20106	N1607B	22234
		I-DEMU	19732	JA8153	22595	LX-OCV	21575	N1608B	22302
HS Thiland		I-DEMV	23301	JA8154	22745	LX-SAL	20116	N16020	19731
		I-DEMW	23476	JA8155	22746	LX-TAP	22169	N171UA	24322
HS-TGA	21782			JA8156	22709			N17125	20271
HS-TGB	21783	**JA Japan**		JA8157	22710	**N United States**		N17126	20273
HS-TGC	21784			JA8158	22711			N172UA	24363
HS-TGD	22472	JA8101	19725	JA8159	22712	N10023	20012	N173UA	24380
HS-TGF	22337	JA8102	19736	JA8160	22989	N10024	20534	N174UA	24381
HS-TGG	22471	JA8103	19727	JA8160	21744	N116KB	23027	N1780B	21515
HS-TGJ	23721	JA8104	19823	JA8161	22990	N117KC	23028	N1781B	23071
HS-TGS	22472	JA8105	19824	JA8162	22991	N118KD	23029	N1781B	23150
HS-TGV	23722	JA8106	19825	JA8163	23067	N119KE	23030	N1783B	21255
HS-VGB	19744	JA8107	20332	JA8163	23149	N120KF	23031	N1783B	22479
HS-VGF	19745	JA8108	20333	JA8164	23068	N121KG	23032	N1784B	22705
HS-VGG	20399	JA8109	20503	JA8164	23150	N122KH	23033	N1784B	23070
		JA8110	20504	JA8165	21743	N123KJ	23243	N1784B	23222
HZ Saudi Arabia		JA8111	20505	JA8166	23151	N1239NE	21251	N1785B	21516
		JA8112	20528	JA8167	23138	N124KK	23244	N1786B	21220
HZ-AIA	22498	JA8113	20529	JA8168	23139	N1248E	21468	N1786B	23151
HZ-AIB	22499	JA8114	20530	JA8169	23389	N125KL	23245	N1789B	21725
HZ-AIC	22500	JA8115	20531	JA8170	23390	N1252E	21537	N1790B	21238
HZ-AID	22501	JA8116	20532	JA8171	23391	N1252E	21731	N1791B	21189
HZ-AIE	22502	JA8117	20781	JA8172	23348	N1288E	21688	N1794B	20373
HZ-AIF	22503	JA8118	20782	JA8173	23482	N1288E	21832	N1794B	20801
HZ-AIG	22747	JA8119	20783	JA8174	23501	N1289E	21833	N1795B	20781
HZ-AIH	22748	JA8120	20784	JA8175	23502	N1289E	22272	N1795B	20237
HZ-AII	22749	JA8121	20923			N1290E	21834	N1796B	19730
HZ-AIJ	22750	JA8122	20924	**JY Jordan**		N1290E	22107	N1796B	20771
HZ-AIK	23262	JA8123	21034			N1295E	22376	N1798B	20770
HZ-AIL	23263	JA8124	21032	JY-AFA	21251	N1298E	22379	N1799B	19761
HZ-AIM	23264	JA8125	21030	JY-AFB	21252	N1298E	22380	N1799B	20704
HZ-AIN	23265	JA8126	21033	JY-AFS	22579	N1301E	22302	N17010	19729
HZ-AIO	23266	JA8127	21031			N1301E	22302	N17011	19730
HZ-AIP	23267	JA8128	21029	**LN Norway**		N1304E	21934	N1800B	19746
HZ-AIQ	23268	JA8129	21678			N1304TW	20117	N1800B	20530
HZ-AIR	23269	JA8130	21679	LN-AEO	20121	N1305E	22428	N18815	20887
						N1309E	22380		

N202AE	21097	N4723U	19882	N601BN	20207	N607PE	20011	N671UP	20323
N203AE	21098	N4727U	19883	N6018N	22791	N607US	19784	N672UP	20324
N204AE	21099	N4728U	19925	N6018N	24067	N608BN	22302	N673UP	20325
N211JL	22989	N4729U	19926	N601BN	23389	N608PE	20012	N674UP	20100
N212JL	23067	N4732U	19927	N6108N	23221	N608US	19785	N675UP	20390
N213JL	23068	N4735U	19928	N6108N	23301	N609BN	22235	N676UP	20101
N221GE	22995	N480GX	19746	N6108N	23480	N609PE	20534	N701SW	20826
N221GF	22996	N50022	20011	N601US	19778	N609US	19786	N702SW	20827
N247SP	21023	N529PA	21992	N602BN	20208	N610BN	19746	N703SW	20828
N26861	19733	N530PA	21022	N602BN	21682	N610PE	20535	N703SW	21764
N26862	19734	N531PA	21023	N602FF	19734	N610US	19787	N704SW	21841
N26863	19735	N532PA	21024	N602PE	21682	N611BN	20527	N705SW	22150
N26864	20305	N533PA	21025	N602US	19779	N611PE	19732	N706SW	22151
N28366	20800	N534PA	21026	N603BN	21785	N611US	20356	N723PA	21439
N28888	20542	N535PA	20651	N603FF	19746	N612BN	22236	N724PA	21316
N28899	20543	N535PA	21027	N603PE	19729	N612US	20357	N725PA	19898
N28903	20541	N536PA	21028	N603US	19780	N613US	20358	N726PA	21048
N301TW	20501	N536PA	21441	N6038E	23269	N614US	20359	N727PA	21162
N302TW	20502	N537PA	21547	N6038E	23287	N615US	20360	N728PA	20712
N303TW	20116	N538PA	21548	N6038E	23509	N616US	21120	N729PA	20713
N304TW	20117	N539PA	21648	N6038N	23271	N617US	21121	N730PA	20888
N305TW	20742	N53110	19676	N604BN	21786	N618US	21122	N731PA	19637
N342SP	21024	N53111	19677	N604GP	23270	N619US	21321	N732PA	19638
N351AS	21785	N53112	19678	N604GP	23611	N620BN	20927	N733PA	19640
N354AS	21189	N53115	20320	N604GP	23621	N620US	19918	N734PA	19641
N355AS	19729	N53116	20321	N604GP	23622	N621US	19919	N735PA	19642
N356AS	19730	N540PA	21649	N604GP	23721	N622US	21704	N736PA	19643
N357AS	19731	N5573B	23120	N604PE	19731	N623US	21705	N737PA	19644
N358AS	19732	N5573B	23149	N604US	19781	N624US	21706	N738PA	19645
N359AS	20520	N5573B	24061	N6046	22750	N625US	21707	N739PA	19646
N371EA	20012	N5573F	22481	N6046P	23139	N626US	21708	N740PA	19647
N33021	20520	N5573K	22991	N6046P	23264	N627US	21709	N740Q	20080
N40108	19896	N5573P	23223	N6046P	22750	N628US	22389	N7402Q	20081
N40116	21141	N57202	21962	N6046P	22490	N629US	22388	N7403Q	20082
N41035	21025	N57203	21963	N6046P	23265	N630US	21668	N7404Q	20083
N4501Q	22381	N58201	21961	N6046P	23393	N631US	23111	N741PA	19648
N4502R	22496	N603BN	21785	N605BN	21991	N632US	23112	N741PR	21832
N4506H	22794	N6005C	22704	N605PE	20520	N633US	21991	N7410Q	20080
N4508E	22678	N6005C	23224	N605US	19782	N63305	20799	N7411TV	21964
N4508H	22547	N6005C	23262	N6055X	23267	N634US	22234	N742PA	19649
N4522V	22805	N6005C	23266	N6055X	23286	N635US	21682	N742PR	21833
N45224	20520	N6005C	23268	N6055X	23408	N638US	23549	N742TV	21965
N4544F	22939	N6005C	23392	N6055X	23501	N6500C	22616	N743PA	19650
N4548M	23056	N6005C	23394	N6055X	24158	N652PA	20347	N743PR	21834
N4551N	23137	N6005C	23407	N6055X	23508	N653PA	20348	N743TV	22403
N4703U	19753	N6005C	23439	N606BN	21992	N654PA	20349	N744PA	19651
N4704U	19754	N6005C	23688	N606PE	19730	N655PA	20350	N744PR	22382
N4710U	19755	N6005C	24062	N606US	19783	N656PA	20351	N744TV	22404
N4711U	19756	N6005C	24138	N6065Y	23409	N657PA	20352	N745TV	22405
N4712U	19757	N6005F	23348	N60659	23502	N658PA	20353	N747AV	19734
N4713U	19875	N6006C	23026	N6066U	22472	N659PA	20354	N747BA	19734
N4714U	19876	N6009F	22489	N6066U	23048	N661US	23719	N747BA	20770
N4716U	19877	N6009F	23263	N6066Z	23138	N662AA	20101	N747BC	20771
N4717U	19878	N6009F	23300	N6066B	23461	N662US	23720	N747BC	21048
N4718U	19879	N6009F	23390	N6066B	23722	N663US	23818	N747BH	21162
N4719U	19880	N6009F	23395	N6067B	22870	N664US	23819	N747BJ	21316
N472EV	20302	N6009F	23676	N6069D	22487	N665US	23820	N747BK	21439
N4720U	19881	N6009F	23482	N607BN	22234	N666US	23821	N747BL	19732

Reg	c/n	Reg	c/n	Reg	c/n	Reg	c/n	Reg	c/n
N747BM	20011	N8279V	23026	N9898	19898	PP-VNC	22107	VH-ECA	21354
N747BN	20012	N8280V	22305	N9899	20246	PP-VNH	23394	VH-ECB	21977
N747FT	20712	N8281V	22486	N9900	20247	PP-VNI	23395	VH-ECC	22615
N747PA	19639	N8281V	22498					VH-OJA	24354

OD Lebanon

SE Sweden

VR Hong Kong

Reg	c/n	Reg	c/n	Reg	c/n	Reg	c/n	Reg	c/n
N747QC	19639	N8284V	21991						
N747SP	21022	N8285V	21241	OD-AGC	20391	SE-DDL	20120	VR-HIA	21966
N747TA	20712	N8285V	22234	OD-AGH	21097	SE-DFZ	21575	VR-HIB	22149
N747WA	20651	N8286V	21604	OD-AGI	21098			VR-HIC	22429
N747WR	20651	N8289V	22969	OD-AGJ	21099			VR-HID	22530
N7470	20235	N8289V	19735	OD-AGM	20390	SU Egypt		VR-HIE	22872
N748FT	20713	N8291V	21589					VR-HIF	23048
N748PA	19652	N8293V	21514			SU-GAK	20117	VR-HIH	23120
N748TA	20713	N8295V	21352	OO Belgium				VR-HII	23221
N748WA	20652	N8296V	22614			SX Greece		VR-HIJ	23392
N749FT	20888	N8296V	22764	OO-SGA	20401			VR-HKG	21746
N749PA	19653	N8196V	22971	OO-SGB	20402	SX-OAA	20742	VR-HVY	22306
N749R	20013	N8297V	20977	OO-SGC	23439	SX-OAB	20825		
N749TA	20888	N8297V	21111			SX-OAC	21683	VT India	
N749WA	20653	N88931	20798	OY Denmark		SX-OAD	21684		
N750PA	19654	N901PA	20391			SX-OAE	21935	VT-EBD	19959
N750WA	19733	N902PA	19896	OY-KFA	20121			VT-EBE	19960
N751PA	19655	N903PA	20100	OY-KHA	20121	TJ Cameroon		VT-EBN	20459
N752PA	19656	N904PA	21743	OY-KHB	22381			VT-EBO	20558
N753PA	19657	N905NA	20107			TJ-CAB	22378	VT-EDU	21182
N754PA	19658	N905PA	21744	PH Netherlands				VT-EFJ	21446
N755PA	19659	N93101	19667			TU Ivory Coast		VT-EFO	21473
N770PA	19660	N93102	19668	PH-BFA	23999			VT-EFU	21829
N771PA	19661	N93103	19669	PH-BFB	24000	TU-TAP	22169	VT-EGA	21993
N77772	19918	N93104	19670	PH-BUA	19922			VT-EGB	21994
N77773	19919	N93105	19671	PH-BUB	19923	VH Australia		VT-EGC	21995
N780T	19746	N93106	19672	PH-BUC	19924			VT-ENQ	21436
N800FT	20100	N93107	19673	PH-BUD	20398	VH-EAA	22495		
N800U	20208	N93108	19674	PH-BUE	20399	VH-EAB	22672	YI Iraqi	
N801FT	20101	N93109	19675	PH-BUF	20400	VH-EBA	20009		
N802FT	20323	N93113	20080	PH-BUG	20427	VH-EBB	20010	YI-AGN	21180
N803FT	19897	N93114	20081	PH-BUH	21110	VH-EBC	20011	YI-AGO	21181
N804FT	20246	N93115	20320	PH-BUI	21111	VH-EBD	20012	YI-AGP	22366
N805FT	20247	N93118	20082	PH-BUK	21549	VH-EBE	20534	YI-ALM	22858
N806FT	21827	N93119	20083	PH-BUL	21550	VH-EBF	20535		
N807FT	21828	N9661	20100	PH-BUM	21659	VH-EBG	20841	YK Syria	
N808FT	22245	N9662	20101	PH-BUN	21660	VH-EBH	20842		
N809FT	19733	N9663	20102	PH-BUO	21848	VH-EBI	20921	YK-AHA	21174
M809FT	22237	N9664	20103	PH-BUX	23508	VH-EBJ	21054	YK-AHB	21175
N810FT	22237	N9665	20104	PH-MCE	23652	VH-EBK	21140		
N811FT	20826	N9666	20105			VH-EBL	21237	ZK New Zealand	
N812FT	20827	N9667	20106	PH Indonesia		VH-EBM	21352		
N813FT	21764	N9668	20107			VH-EBN	21353	ZK-NZV	22722
N184FT	21841	N9669	20108	PK-GSA	22246	VH-EBO	21657	ZK-NZW	22723
N815FT	22150	N9670	20109	PK-GSB	22247	VH-EBP	21658	ZK-NZX	22724
N816FT	22151	N9671	20323	PK-GSC	22248	VH-EBQ	22145	ZK-NZY	22725
N817FT	20349	N9672	20324	PK-GSD	22249	VH-EBR	22614	ZK-NZZ	22791
N818FT	20353	N9673	20325	PK-GSE	22768	VH-EBS	22616		
N819FT	19661	N9674	20326	PK-GSF	22769	VH-EBT	22617	ZS South Africa	
N820FT	20391	N9675	20390			VH-EBT	23222		
N8277V	21507	N9676	20391	PP Brasil		VH-EBU	23223	ZS-SAA	22170
N8277V	22704	N9676	20101			VH-EBV	23224	ZS-SAB	22171
N8278V	22870	N9896	19896	PP-VNA	22105	VH-EBW	23408		
N8279V	22970	N9897	19897	PP-VNB	22106	VH-EBX	23688		

ZS-SAL	20273				5-291	19735
ZS-SAM	20238	9M-MHI	22304		5-8101	19667
ZS-SAN	20239	9M-MHJ	22442		5-8102	19678
ZS-SAO	20556				5-8103	20080
ZS-SAP	20557	9Q Zaire			5-8104	19677
ZS-SAR	22170				5-8105	20081
ZS-SAS	22171	9Q-ARW	19637		5-8106	19668
ZS-SAT	22970	9Q-CKF	20829		5-8107	20082
ZS-SAU	22971				5-8108	19669
ZS-SPA	21132	9V Singapore			5-8109	20083
ZS-SPB	21133				5-8110	19733
ZS-SPC	21134	9V-SIA	20712		5-8111	19734
ZS-SPD	21253	9V-SIB	20713		5-8112	19735
ZS-SPE	21254	9V-SKA	23026		5-8113	21486
ZS-SPF	21263	9V-SKB	23027		5-8114	21487
		9V-SKC	23028		5-8115	21507
3B Mauritius		9V-SKD	23029		5-8116	21514
		9V-SKE	23030			
3B-NAG	21134	9V-SKF	23031		United States	
		9V-SKG	23032			
4R Sri Lanka		9V-SKH	23033		73-01676	20682
		9V-SKM	23049		73-01677	20683
4R-ULF	20009	9V-SKN	23410		74-00787	20684
4R-ULG	20010	9V-SKP	23246		75-00125	20949
		9V-SMA	24061			
4X Israel		9V-SMB	24062			
		9V-SQC	20888			
4X-AXA	20135	9V-SQD	21048			
4X-AXB	20274	9V-SQE	21162			
4X-AXC	20704	9V-SQF	21316			
4X-AXD	21190	9V-SQG	21439			
4X-AXF	21594	9V-SQH	21683			
4X-AXG	21737	9V-SQI	21684			
4X-AXH	22254	9V-SQJ	21935			
4X-AXZ	19735	9V-SQK	21936			
		9V-SQL	21937			
5A Lybia		9V-SQM	21938			
		9V-SQN	21939			
5A-DIJ	22105	9V-SQO	21940			
5A-DIK	22106	9V-SQP	21941			
5A-DIL	22107	9V-SQQ	21942			
		9V-SQR	21943			
5R Madagasgar		9V-SQS	21944			
5R-MFT	21614	Military Operated				
7Q Malawi		Iran				
7Q-YKL	21133	5-280	19667			
		5-281	19678			
9K Kuwait		5-282	19668			
		5-282	20080			
9K-ADA	21541	5-283	19677			
9K-ADB	21542	5-284	20081			
9K-ADC	21543	5-286	20082			
9K-ADD	22740	5-287	19669			
		5-289	19733			
9M Malaysia		5-290	19734			

Key to abbreviations

reg = registration
s/n = serial (or construction) number
ff = first flown
dd = date delivered
NTU = not taken up
w/o = written off

Index

Other Bestsellers of Related Interest

GENERAL AVIATION LAW—Jerry A. Eichenberger

Although the regulatory burden that is part of flying sometimes seems overwhelming, it need not take the pleasure out of your flight time. Eichenberger provides an up-to-date survey of many aviation regulations, and gives you a solid understanding of FAA procedures and functions, airman ratings and maintenance certificates, the implications of aircraft ownership, and more. This book will allow you to recognize legal problems before they result in FAA investigations and the potentially serious consequences. 240 pages. Book No. 3431, $16.95 paperback, $25.95 hardcover

THE JOY OF FLYING—2nd Editon
—Robert Mark

Here are the answers to just about every question a nonflyer could have about flying. From practical information to humorous sidelights, Mark covers what it's like to be behind the controls of an aircraft, the ins and outs of pilot training, techniques for communicating with air traffic control, reasons and requirements for advanced pilot ratings, even the ten greatest lies to tell a nonflying spouse. It's a fascinating and fun-filled look at the pleasures, challenges, and requirements of learning to pilot an airplane. 176 pages, 67 illustrations. Book No. 2444, $14.95 paperback only

THE PILOT'S RADIO COMMUNICATIONS HANDBOOK—3rd Edition
—Paul E. Illman and Jay Pouzar
"*. . . should have a spot on your bookshelf . . .*"
                                        —*Private Pilot*
"*. . . time spent on this book is sure to make your flight smoother.*"   —*Kitplanes*
An updated edition of a popular handbook. Contains information on FAA rule changes regarding Mode C transponders, single-class TCA operations, and student pilot TCA training requirements. Current issues relating to the entire spectrum of VFR radio communications are addressed. Now, you can use even the busiest airports with confidence and skill. 240 pages, 61 illustrations. Book No. 2445, $15.95 paperback only

MASTERING INSTRUMENT FLYING
—Henry Sollman with Sherwood Harris

Mastering Instrument Flying introduces an entirely new course designed from beginning to end to meet or exceed the Instrument Flight Test standards recently published by the FAA. The elements, techniques, procedures, and tolerances of instrument flight are addressed in precise detail. Illustrated information on how to prepare for the instrument flight test is provided, and additional advanced procedures not specifically required for the instrument rating are covered. 336 pages, 256 illustrations. Book No. 2433, $18.95 paperback only

IMPROVE YOUR FLYING SKILLS:
Tips from a Pro—Donald J. Clausing

Learn firsthand the professional attitudes, flying standards, and everyday procedures practiced by airline and corporate aircraft captains. Leading off with an overview of the basics of flying VFR and IFR, the author gives in-depth coverage of all the things that make up advanced, no-nonsense airmanship. Among the topics covered: flight planning, cruise control, types of approaches, weather flying, filing IFR, radio procedures, and "BILAHS" (Briefing, IFR, Log, Alternate, Hazardous weather). 224 pages, 42 illustrations. Book No. 3328, $14.95 paperback, $24.95 hardcover

UNCONVENTIONAL AIRCRAFT—2nd Edition
—Peter M. Bowers

From one of America's foremost aviation photographers and historians comes what is probably the largest collection of information on unconventional aircraft ever assembled. Far-out flying machines that have appeared in the last 80 years receive their due honor, humor, and respect in this salute to them and their creators. For this revised and expanded edition, Bowers has added 77 additional aircraft, including the Rutan Voyager, Beechcraft Starship, the Bell/Boeing V-22 Osprey tilt-rotor VTOL, and the Zeppelin-Staaken R-IV bomber. 336 pages, 437 illustrations. Book No. 2450, $19.95 paperback, $28.95 hardcover

THE ILLUSTRATED GUIDE TO AERODYNAMICS—Hubert "Skip" Smith

If you've always considered aerodynamic science a highly technical area best left to professional engineers and aircraft designers . . . this outstanding new sourcebook will change your mind! Smith introduces the principles of aerodynamics to everyone who wants to know how and why aircraft fly . . . but who doesn't want to delve into exotic theories or complicated mathematical relationships. 240 pages, 232 illustrations. Book No. 2390, $17.95 paperback only

MAYDAY, MAYDAY, MAYDAY! Spin Instructions Please—Bob Stevens

Pilots, aviation buffs, and anyone with a sense of humor will enjoy this all-new collection of cartoons created by the undisputed Dean of American Aviation Cartooning, Bob Stevens. Poking fun at every aspect of general aviation, from soloing to flying the airways (and battling the bureaucracy) to the inevitable hangar flying, *Mayday* doesn't disappoint. 224 pages, Illustrated. Book No. 28964, $12.95 paperback only

MORE I LEARNED ABOUT FLYING FROM THAT—Editors of *Flying®* Magazine

What would you do if you lost half your wing in a midair collision or a strike force of wasps attacked you in the cockpit at 3,000 feet? What pilots have actually done in these nightmarish situations and in dozens of others is told by the fliers themselves in this gathering of accounts from *Flying* magazine's popular "I Learned About Flying From That" column. This is a treasury of unforgettable true tales and incisive pointers that save you from learning about flying the hard way. 196 pages. Book No. 3317, $12.95 paperback only

AVOIDING COMMON PILOT ERRORS: An Air Traffic Controller's View—John Stewart

A pilot, flight instructor, and air traffic controller of 20 years' experience cites examples of recurring pilot error. Improper training, lack of preflight preparations, poor communication skills, and confusing regulations are among the problems discussed. 240 pages, Illustrated. Book No. 2434, $16.95 paperback only

Aero Series, Vol. 33, THE McDONNELL DOUGLAS APACHE—Frank Colucci

Go behind the scenes to learn about this aircraft's maximum combat capabilities of night vision, stealth, agility, survivability, firepower, and attack. The craft's tested performance capabilities dramatically exceed specified requirements in target detection, acquisition, tracking recognition and identification with direct-view optics, television, and forward-looking infra-red sensors. 112 pages, more than 100 photos, 8-page color section. Book No. 20614, $10.95 paperback only

AIM/FAR 1990—TAB/AERO Staff

Unsurpassed by any other in the industry, this pilot resource features New FAR Part 91 Rules—Complete and Unabridged—with a summary of proposed versions for easy reference. Federal regulations that directly impact general aviation, new Recreational Pilot certificate requirements, DUAT information, extensive coverage of Loran-C, and much more. Don't fly without it. 608 pages, Illustrated. Book No. 24390, $11.95 paperback only

GOOD TAKEOFFS AND GOOD LANDINGS —Joe Christy

This reference thoroughly examines single-engine aircraft takeoffs and landings, and the critical transitions accompanying each. The author stresses that every pilot must continually evaluate ever-changing factors of wind, air pressure, precipitation, traffic, temperature, visibility, runway length, and braking conditions. *Good Takeoffs and Good Landings* belongs on every pilot's required reading list. 192 pages, 70 illustrations. Book No. 2487, $14.95 paperback only

LEARJETS: The World's Executive Aircraft —Donald J. Porter

Air industry veteran Donald Porter tells the riveting inside story of the evolution, development, production, and flight performance of the Learjet series. He traces the complete history of the Lear jets from concept and design to current production methods. Breathtaking photographs round out the volume. Whether you value a well-told story or need on a particular Learjet specification, this belongs on your bookshelf—or in your hangar! 128 pages, 32 illustrations. Book No. 2440, $11.95 paperback only

Aero Series, Vol. 37, BOEING 737
—David H. Minton

This book offers an accurate and complete historical record of the Boeing 737, including commercial uses, prototypes, variations, and military applications. More than 100 line drawings and photographs illustrate the 737 from every possible angle, showing details on wings, tails, engines, pylons, cockpit interiors, galleys, instruments, cabin layouts, and liveries in close-up detail. Includes a detailed scale modeler's section and eight pages of full-color photographs. 80 pages, 8-page full-color insert. Book No. 20618, $10.95 paperback only

Aero Series, Vol. 39, A-7 CORSAIR II
—William G. Holder

Nicknamed "SLUF" (for Short Little Ugly Fello the A-7 Corsair II has received more than it share of ver jabs—this in spite of performing its job better than poss bly any other aircraft in military history. This tells th complete story of the A-7 Corsair II, from its inception i the mid-1960s to its present use, and details the aircraft's technical aspects, developmental phases, modifications, and combat history. 96 pages, 78 illustrations, 8 color pages. Book No. 3452, $10.95 paperback only

Prices Subject to Change Without Notice.

Look for These and Other TAB Books at Your Local Bookstore

To Order Call Toll Free 1-800-822-8158

(in PA, AK, and Canada call 717-794-2191)

or write to TAB BOOKS, Blue Ridge Summit, PA 17294-0840.

Title		Product No.	Quantity	Price

☐ Check or money order made payable to TAB BOOKS

Charge my ☐ VISA ☐ MasterCard ☐ American Express

Acct. No. _____ Exp. _____

Signature: _____

Name: _____

Address: _____

City: _____

State: _____ Zip: _____

Subtotal $ _____

Postage and Handling
($3.00 in U.S., $5.00 outside U.S.) $ _____

Add applicable state and local
sales tax $ _____

TOTAL $ _____

TAB BOOKS catalog free with purchase; otherwise send $1.00 in check or money order and receive $1.00 credit on your next purchase.

Orders outside U.S. must pay with international money order in U.S. dollars.

TAB Guarantee: If for any reason you are not satisfied with the book(s) you order, simply return it (them) within 15 days and receive a full refund.   **BC**

w),
bal
si-
e

Aero Series, Vol. 37, BOEING 737
—David H. Minton

This book offers an accurate and complete historical record of the Boeing 737, including commercial uses, prototypes, variations, and military applications. More than 100 line drawings and photographs illustrate the 737 from every possible angle, showing details on wings, tails, engines, pylons, cockpit interiors, galleys, instruments, cabin layouts, and liveries in close-up detail. Includes a detailed scale modeler's section and eight pages of full-color photographs. 80 pages, 8-page full-color insert. Book No. 20618, $10.95 paperback only

Aero Series, Vol. 39, A-7 CORSAIR II
—William G. Holder

Nicknamed "SLUF" (for Short Little Ugly Fellow), the A-7 Corsair II has received more than it share of verbal jabs—this in spite of performing its job better than possibly any other aircraft in military history. This tells the complete story of the A-7 Corsair II, from its inception in the mid-1960s to its present use, and details the aircraft's technical aspects, developmental phases, modifications, and combat history. 96 pages, 78 illustrations, 8 color pages. Book No. 3452, $10.95 paperback only

Prices Subject to Change Without Notice.

Look for These and Other TAB Books at Your Local Bookstore

To Order Call Toll Free 1-800-822-8158
(in PA, AK, and Canada call 717-794-2191)

or write to TAB BOOKS, Blue Ridge Summit, PA 17294-0840.

Title		Product No.	Quantity	Price

☐ Check or money order made payable to TAB BOOKS

Charge my ☐ VISA ☐ MasterCard ☐ American Express

Acct. No. _____ Exp. _____

Signature: _____

Name: _____

Address: _____

City: _____

State: _____ Zip: _____

Subtotal $ _____

Postage and Handling
($3.00 in U.S., $5.00 outside U.S.) $ _____

Add applicable state and local
sales tax $ _____

TOTAL $ _____

TAB BOOKS catalog free with purchase; otherwise send $1.00 in check or money order and receive $1.00 credit on your next purchase.

Orders outside U.S. must pay with international money order in U.S. dollars.

TAB Guarantee: If for any reason you are not satisfied with the book(s) you order, simply return it (them) within 15 days and receive a full refund.
BC